ISBN: 9798751793630

DEDICATION

Dedicated to the wonderful community of poets I discovered on Instagram; a worldwide community of diversity, that is constantly growing, evolving, and thriving. You are the lighthouses that bring my ship to shore. You are part of my daily life, and I treasure you daily.

And to all aspiring poets and writers everywhere; I hope this book, and ongoing project, fills you up and inspires you to new heights.

Yours always,

Ryan Daniel Warner

FOREWORD

The poetry that follows in this; the September 2021 edition of Poetry 365, is a result of the hard work of 73 poets from around the globe; many who have never had work published before. This book serves as an outlet and opening for their talent. The poetry contained within this anthology was originally submitted for my poetry prompts featured on my Instagram account, and I felt this work deserved more exposure than the platform allowed.

In the grand scheme of things; in a world where we are still witnessing the horrifying effects of a virus, where we are seeing severe reminders of segregation and oppression against multiple groups of people, where conflict and cruelty continue to dominate in regions like Afghanistan, Yemen, Sudan, Ethiopia, and the Middle East, and where women continue to fight for equality, I continue to have very little time for pristine textbook level perfection. It means so little in comparison. What does matter to me, and should matter to you; the reader, is the clarity of the messages portrayed in these pieces. The 250 or so pieces I have chosen to be included, out of the many pieces that were submitted, were selected, because, above all else, they tell stories and relay messages exceptionally well, through their flow and voice, enabling us to connect with the hearts and minds of the poets involved, and in doing so, reconnect with parts of ourselves.

Yes, this book may be a little rough around the edges in some ways. Hell, so am I. And so are you, whenever you truthfully look in a mirror. It's what makes us who we are. A few of these poems may have the odd spelling mistake or grammatical error, and some of them may be less well designed than others, but they are all authentic messages, which we need in this day in age. They contain the powerful, inspiring reminders that we need to take action – be that to try and change others, to change the status quo, or to change ourselves. They remind us to love, to seek peace; and to always fight for what we believe in. They remind us to listen to ourselves rather than naysayers.

This is poetry. One day at a time. 365 days of the year.
By those who previously didn't have a voice. By those who matter most.

CONTENTS

KABUL

 z.b.sayed ·

Kabul

The beauty of Kabul is unmatched
It is truly picturesque, in every aspect.

An in built magnet, it has
Attracts attention, mostly bad.

Invaders and empires have ruled this land
But never have they respected Kabul's grants.

The dusty hills of Kabul once stood tall
Today all you see on them are blood and scars.

The city has now given up
It has been time and again used by the corrupt.

Whoever it welcomed has betrayed it's trust
Hurt it's mother's, father's, daughter's and son's.

With a tragic past and a heavy heart
I really hope Kabul will someday make fresh start.

Z.B. Sayed

 mysticlovepoetry ·

THE LOUD CRY

WE SEE TEARS IN GAYA'S EYES, HORRIFIED, HEARING HER CHILDREN CRY.

THE WORLD IS FALLING APART, ARE WE STILL HUMAN OR HAVE WE FALLEN PREY TO THE DEMONS IN OUR HEARTS.

GAYA BLEEDS IN RED FOR US, WATCHING THE ABRUPT EXODUS. FOR THOSE OF US LEFT BEHIND, IT'S A NIGHTMARE ON REPLAY.

DID WE DESERVE TO BE ABANDONED THIS WAY? WHAT IF YOU WERE IN OUR PLACE INSTEAD?

THE FEAR, SUFFERING AND PAIN WILL NOT SUBSIDE. IF THE END IS NIGH, WE CAN ONLY PRAY.
A MIRACLE TO TAKE THIS EVIL AWAY.

MYSTIC LOVE

 emm_kay0 ·

⋮

WRAPPED IN A VEIL AS A SHROUD WRAPS THE REMAINS
OF ONE LONG GONE YET THE STAIN OF BLOOD CLOUDS
THE SKY FOR IT LIES BLEEDING IN THE MAIN STREET
KABUL LIES DYING
NOW DEAD
DEAD AND SILENT
WORDS BLEED IN MEMORY OF A FADING YESTERDAY IN A
WORLD OF NO TOMORROW
THE SILENCE BROKEN BY A MURMUR
INTERMITTENT INTELLECTUAL PROTESTS
A DRY EYED CRYING
WE OFFER PLATITUDES OVER ENDLESS CUPS OF COFFEE
'HOW TERRIBLE!' 'IT SHOULDN'T HAVE HAPPENED!' 'BREAKS
MY HEART!' 'WHAT CAN WE DO!'
OVER AND OVER AGAIN.
DOING NOTHING.
EMM_KAY

noraravenspeaks ·   ⋮

Fear
Upheaval
Mass hysteria
Upending of power
A dark coup overnight
Darkness that feeds on light
Choosing death to leave death behind
Falling to concrete graves from blue skies
Hope snuffed out by a heartless wind
Fluttering flag, ragged, tattered
Worn down, torn within
The color of violence
Blood red aflame
Desolation
Fear

Color me red
-Nora Raven

crystallotus759 ⋅

⋮

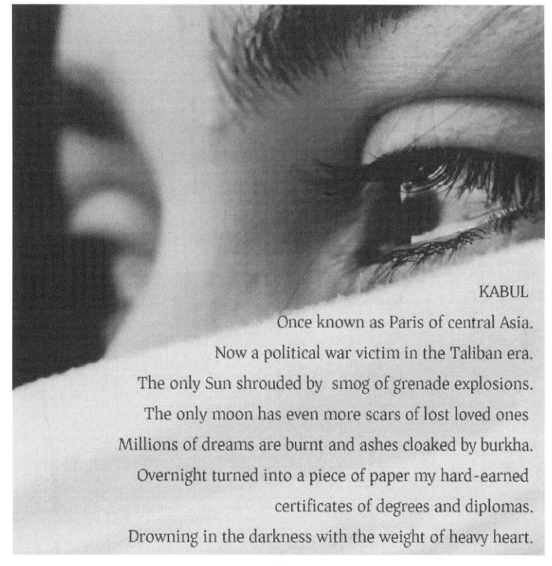

KABUL

Once known as Paris of central Asia.

Now a political war victim in the Taliban era.

The only Sun shrouded by smog of grenade explosions.

The only moon has even more scars of lost loved ones

Millions of dreams are burnt and ashes cloaked by burkha.

Overnight turned into a piece of paper my hard-earned

certificates of degrees and diplomas.

Drowning in the darkness with the weight of heavy heart.

 poetry_in_moments_ ⋅ ⋮

Kabul

Deep down the woods,
under a tall tree,
there lived a thousand bees,
all roaming free,
on spring days, all over the field,
the nectars rich, under a shield,
the place like home, all one and warm,
tasted heaven, and lived a charm,
until one day, a white wolf howled,
eyes deep as night,all fiery and fouled,
one by one, the treasures lost,
hovering around, to watch what it cost,
a slow burn fire, a far watch cry,
with brothers tied, the nest ran dry,
as seasons passed, it tasted sour,
with melted gold, away and far,
a broken home, no wings to fly,
the wolf fed up, as it ran by.

debbie_o_bottled_up_feelings ·

THEY LEFT THEM BEHIND IN KABUL
THEY LEFT THEM THEIR GUNS

AND THEIR PLANES

AMMUNITION THEY DIDN'T HIDE
ALL OF THOSE LIVES GONE

AND WHY?

BECAUSE OF ALL THE SHEEP
FOLLOWING THE DEMENTED THIEF

THE COMMANDER IN CHIEF

THEY LEFT THEM TO DIE IN KABUL

GOD HELP THEM ALL AND GOD HELP

THE US OF A

debbie o' bottled up feelings

 joyshribose ·

KABUL

Betrayed, bruised Kabul in pandemonium,

Horrified, helpless as the world gapes in delirium.

Kabul, the city of beautiful people and culture,

Now a city of panic and fear.

Pathetic sights of residents fleeing the city in despair,

From brutal, barbaric men causing the nightmare.

May the city enveloped with mesmerising mountains

Be freed from this virus in the form of humans.

In which ever name we invoke the Almighty,

May Kabul awake to the new dawn of peace and prosperity.

-JOYSHRI BOSE.

 **israelmgonzalez** ·

YourQuote.in

Four days ago, five days ago
The moon turned to blood
The sun blotted out
It all ended in a rout
They came rushing like a flood

Four days ago, five days ago
Hopes and dreams came crashing down
Like lightning from heaven crashing down
Leaving residues of humanity in the hell below
Caught in a desperation we do not know

Four days, five days ago
The shining city upon a hill grew dark with sorrow
Eclipsed by cynicism for our tomorrow
You see there is no guardian of freedom
And even the grand republic resembles a kingdom

– Izzy Levy

 lishid619 ·

Do you hear your neighbor screaming?

Someone has intruded their home

An aftermath of a land dispute that has been going on for a while

A conflict on history of the soil

A history based on a group of a people in a locality

A history before man learnt to travel

A history before cultures met and traded

A history that never needed to dictate the future

We thought we were safe in our homes

Until the intruders set everything on fire

The heat of which radiated on us

The embers scattered to spread hell

Leaving us no option but to leave our homes

For the devils to deceive their followers towards forged doors of heaven

Behind which everything and everyone were burning down to ground

Behind which no Gods lived

I wonder if the intruders ever stood a chance,

Against a whole neighborhood united irrespective of differences

Homes after homes were burnt down

By one intruder after other with the same story in a new neighborhood

Lishid Mohamed

 **elliemorfou**

KABUL HAS FALLEN

Hear, hear, Kabul is gone!
Format your mind anew.
Unhear the songs of knowledge
dismiss the taste of freedom
untouch the edges of tomorrow's hope
unsee the movie of what your life has been;
go rip your framed degree in two,
cover each trace of your divine nudity.
In my heart, Kabul is a woman whose life has been reset.
She knows what could have been and what is not,
condemned to live her female life concealed at best,
invisible, impermeable by human gaze, illiterate, subordinate;
a fate worse than death.
Kabul, I want to hold your hand
what must I do?

@ELLIEMORFOU

poeticifi

KABUL

Kabul, Kabul
how you have transcended
from glitz and glamour
to fear and frustration
women and children and men
live with fear dancing
in their eyes,
worries in their hearts
uncertainty on their skin
silence on their tongues.
no safehouse is safe enough
when aggrieved criminals are released
no safehouse is safe enough
from voices threatening over the phone.
tossing caution and what-ifs, women take to the
streets
how dare the ones we brought to life
gave our milk
broke our backs for
not give us a chance to live?
how dare the ones we brought to life
gave our milk
broke our backs for
not give us a chance to live?

@poeticifi

@yondaime_flex_an_u

Be wise
Be true
What are you going to do
When your life flashes right before you
The writing has been on the wall at thoughts due
Dreams and aspirations in rue
Crashing down like the Walls of Jericho
Why is it dependent on the West
Why the basic rights of the female is less
Less than the needs of humanity a regress
From all that is earthly even not a test
The fear and despair
Understanding for the western culture corruption no compare
Understanding for the preservation of religious law no
compare
Well...can she at least learn to read and write
Well....can she be given the means of upholding the structure
and principles of the household
Well...can she be given the opportunity to feel
Loved even in your own twisted way
Cherished in the proper religious way
Not interpreted and mismanaged
As an investment
No then
You won't see thousands fleeing for something
Resembling a decent aspect of living
Instead of fighting to breathe
In Kabul

MEDAL OF HONOUR

secret_words_of_hart ·

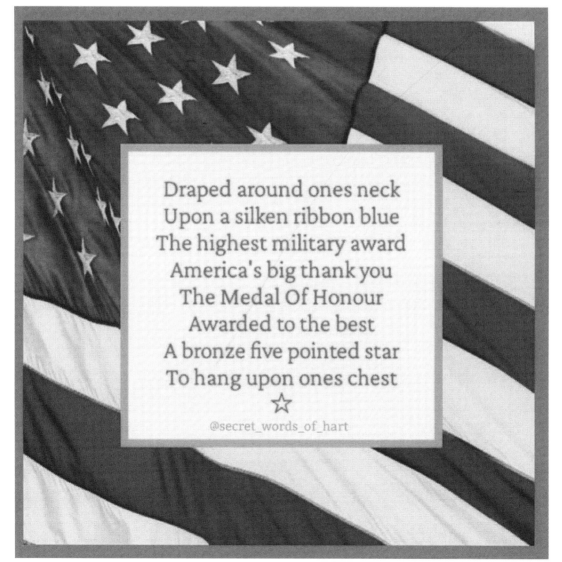

Draped around ones neck
Upon a silken ribbon blue
The highest military award
America's big thank you
The Medal Of Honour
Awarded to the best
A bronze five pointed star
To hang upon ones chest
☆
@secret_words_of_hart

 crystallotus759 ·

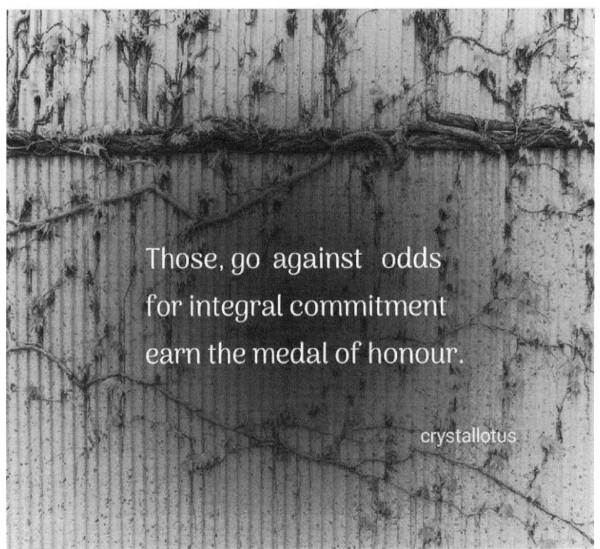

Those, go against odds
for integral commitment
earn the medal of honour.

crystallotus

adanakaz_poetry ·

MEDAL OF HONOUR

Bravery, Courage
America's pride and joy
Nation's gratitude...

Written by Adana
Adanakaz_Poetry

 patriciahelenwriter ·

MEDAL OF HONOUR

No big fanfare.
No celebratory parade.
No television coverage.
No streamers...no hoorays.

In steadfast devotion
in service to community
a core of selfless people
support those facing adversity.

Be they frontline workers
or firefighters or rescue squads
these incredibly brave people
seek neither medals nor applause.

Each deserves a medal of honour.
Each deserves our sincere gratitude
for their acts of true heroism
for the compassion they exude.

@yondaime_flex_an_u

Might fright or flight
Enterprising the heart caught in flight
Down the sky of heaven so bright
Arrayed with courage and discipline
Lined out as soldiers of fortune

Of reactions there is next to none
For this is one rare as the virgin's son

Honorific the least
Opinionated at the very least
Nothing can be negative about this
Only the guts and glory reflecting this
Under the moon
Rising high above the clouds as the sun

MEDAL OF HORROR

secret_words_of_hart ·

 **autumnalfyre ·**

MEDAL OF HORROR

When will I win my medal of horror?
Do I need to douse my story
with some more blood and gore
or is it enough to draw on
the twisted folklore of dark forests
where children don't venture anymore?
Maybe I'm too soft and bright
Maybe I show too much light
and leave my readers a trail of breadcrumbs
to find their way back to safety all right
Maybe I don't want to give you too bad of a fright
just a tiny thrill, a bit of a chill
with a tiny, tidy ghost story
before saying goodnight
Maybe I won't win the medal of horror
but I suppose that's fine

@autumnalfyre

thedarksideofthephoenix ·

thedarksideofthephoenix ·

Tickling my neck, hairs stand to attention,
Creating an unwanted distraction.
I must focus, keep my head in the game,
No one dies because of my mistake.
But who can I trust, who is fake?
Which of these people will abandon me for their own sake,
To save their own skin, leaving me to expire within,
This nightmare, this realm of sin.
Can I blame them? When I am being hunted, what will I do,
Will I abandon them too?
Act with honour, to earn a medal of horror?
Thick air catches in my throat,
Bile rising behind, chasing my breath,
Much like the madman,
Chasing my life, to the death.
Heart thumping violently against my ribs,
Is it my heart or his,
That I hear? Louder, closer, he can sense my fear.
I long to hide, to cower away,
But if I fail to open that gate,
A sacrifice to the entity, shall become my fate...

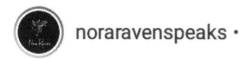

noraravenspeaks ·

⋮

September sings a song
And I ride along
A road trip to paradise
Show me glory before demise
I will wear the medal of honor
Overlaying all prior medals of horror
A road trip to paradise
Show me glory before demise
Leaves turn in the fall
I've given it my all
A road trip to paradise
Show me glory before demise
I've reached the cliff's end
Now its time to take the plunge
A road trip to paradise
Show me glory before demise

September
-Nora Raven

patriciahelenwriter ·

⋮

MEDAL OF HORROR

Vintage Vincent Price and Bela Lugosi
Tom Cruise, Jack Nicholson and Linda Blair-
classic actors who deserve a medal of horror
for starring in movies made of nightmares.

These are some of the pioneers of horror flicks
those 'knuckle-biters'... 'hide-your-eyes' shows
where fanged vampires and those demon
possessed
are featured on cobwebbed sets with deranged
crows.

Mowing down fistfuls of popcorn and screaming
are what terrified members of the audience do.
Nervous energy in the theatre mounts to a peak
watching projectile vomiting and gushy blood
spews.

punkcoffeepoet ·

⋮

Satan half-relinquishes his token

@punkcoffeepoet

I get ear infections of lightheartedness from your
attitude
But at least I have the darkness of millions
I have a vagabond absence of an organ
That you would know nothing about, dear lamb
I also have the answer to all of your mind's
concoctions:
Breath-play for serial killers,
Clarity of conscience
And the one who wins the ice skating competition by
kneeling at the shrine of Dead Ones
Ordinary darlings receive understanding from
knowing the world is in their nimble fingers at the cost
of its unfurling
But only when my destitute Dark Spirit believes upon
a nuanced CEO of heaven's holy-roller-skater's rink
Will I think,
"To you I condone and pass down my most pitch-
matte-black Medal of Horrors!"
(But just know that if such a gem of generational
scares shall be given,
I am not willing to not share first place as your
equivalent.)

 **annawriterspage**

You dreamingly drew me
a portrait of your faking
and you viciously wrote me
a timeline of my breaking.
You hurt the little girl I was,
the bleeding never stopped.
I kissed you like you could fix me
But my happiness had been locked.
It took the earth to orbit the sun
until I loved me wholly,
igniting a riot in my ribcage
to catch up to you slowly.
Smiling, I end this stupid race.
I grab you by your collar.
Been to hell and back now,
I present you your medal of horror.
So if you ever try to crack my heart open again
all you'll find is this inner child of mine,
wearing her revolution in her wounded heart.
Not looking back, she's fine.

                                                    - A.Writer

benjaminsart77

Medal of Horror

@BenjaminsArt77

You feel their joy & pain
The day they made it acid rain
Since there lips last met
Time became their threat
That they soon learned to eliminate
Once near the 9th gate
To begin their moveable feast
With all 4 canine teeth
Kissing the very nature of the beast
Blood in/blood out at the very least
Giving and receiving the Medal of Horror
Behind closed window shades in Bora Bora
Tip toeing on eachothers soul's ledge
Accepting life on the edge

 elliemorfou ·

THE ROMAN EMPEROR

He, who conquered lands.
He, who commanded armies.
He, who knew no superiors.
He. The Roman Emperor.
Powerful Ceasar, Ceasar almighty;
recorded for eternity in the register of history

and yet
if asked to cite three things about him

I'll surely say:
1 - Cleopatra's affair;
2 - Popular chicken salad on a menu;
3 - My least desired childbirth mode.

Boyfriend, salad, butchery.

Oh, mighty warrior!

 z.b.sayed ·

Caesar

A great politician ; A great orator
Yes, I am talking about no one else
Its, Julius Caesar.
Call him a tyrant, an authoritarian or any other
He is the reason for reforms from Roman people to Roman weather

The Julius calendar, the Roman Republic
Was terribly refuted by the elite public
Who wanted no dictator but democracy
In the end Brutus became the cause of civil distress and atrocities.

Caesar was a military man,
Who brought about peace and order in the land.
But how long can a dictator dictate
Among people brew distress and hate
Together they stabbed 23 times
That was the end of Caesars crimes.

Z.B. Sayed

adanakaz_poetry ·

CAESAR

Cleopatra's lover
Politician and Scholar
A Timeless Roman Leader...

Written by Adana
Adanakaz_Poetry

 patriciahelenwriter ·

⋮

CAESAR

"Et tu, Brute?"
are the last words Caesar utters
as his once beloved friend, Brutus
watches him gasp and sputter.
Political corruption and betrayal
ensure Caesar's dictatorship ends
and on this ill-fated Ides of March
Brutus stabs and kills his friend.

@yondaime_flex_an_u

Can you please show
Acclaimed to be true and goes without a delay
Encouraging all that is adventurous and ambitious
Showing the passion for country and your kind
Always looking for a better way
Remembering the best approach regardless of decay

WOMEN AND CHILDREN

sticksandstonespoet ·
Melbourne, Victoria, Austra

I'M SORRY I'M NOT ENOUGH
I'M SORRY I FUCKED UP
I WANT YOU TO KNOW I TRIED
TO DO THE BEST WITH WHAT I HAD
IT'S NOT AN EXCUSE
BUT I WAS DAMAGED TOO
ALL YOU DID WAS GIVE ME PRIDE
EVERYDAY OF OUR LIVES
AND FOR YOU I WOULD HAVE DIED
IN A HEARTBEAT MOMENT
IT BREAKS MY HEART
YOU HAD TO PICK SIDES
NO MOTHER SHOULD BE SEPERATE FROM HER CHILD
JUST TO SURVIVE WITHOUT YOU HERE BY ME
I DELIBERATELY DON'T COUNT THE DAYS
THE CALENDAR MILESTONES
I FIND IT EASIER THAT WAY
NOW YOU ARE MISSING FROM ME
IM JUST ANOTHER MOTHER LIVING IN ABSENTIA

@sticksandstonespoet
©dmccarthy

davydwriter ·
Family History

⋮

Fish is Expensive.

We are the masters of light, bringing in the anticipation of a cool breeze. Old beams drip with sensations of sour milk. We must be thankful. Remember the surprise of a warm handshake, or the drunkenness brought with a five-a.m. alarm.

Mam was outraged when she caught us licking windows. We were tickled pink, whilst she stood there looking all perplexed, threatening us with the horror of soap suds. In a way she was right.

You preferred the relief brought by fizzing sherbet on your tongue, bursting with excitement at the opening page of a new book and fresh adventure. I was more wrapped up in the thrill of a last-minute penalty and being dangled over Saltom Cliffs looking for Herring Gull eggs.

 **davydwriter** ⋅
Family History

⋮

We were so different, yet she was full of love for both of us, always embracing your calm and my rage and mayhem.

You warmed her with Treasure Island, I reddened mam's cheeks with muddy boots across her kitchen floor.

Either way, there was still thankfulness written inside her laughter.

DavyD

 patriciahelenwriter ·

WOMEN AND CHILDREN

Women ... vessels of strength ...
women ... nurturers and protectors
tirelessly stoke in their children
tiny sparks of hope for the future.

Children ... filled light and love ...
children ... filled with optimism
eagerly rise to the challenges
of a troubled world.

Women and children.

yondaime_flex_an_u
Love Is Love

You are the reason
The world spins every single day
The motivation in all walks of life
To always do better
To push through when things are rougher

yondaime_flex_an_u
Love Is Love

To embrace change when its uglier
In times when it never looks better
You are the prize
You are the comfort
You are the happiness
You are the base of love

yondaime_flex_an_u
Love Is Love

⋮

You are the attachment like above
Heavenly to the core the feeling behove
One and only to see how important
Women make life worthy to experience
Children humble our hearts beyond convenience

THE GRUDGE

novamarie_poetry · ⋮

I'd love to say that
I don't hold grudges.
But, here I am
with my hands full
of viscous memories,
sticky on my fingers.
I bring them to my mouth
and taste.
Bitter.

@novamarie_poetry   9/25/2021

poetry_ordeal_solitude_solace_ ·

Grudge

This story dates way back
When my fingers couldn't bear paint marks
And my lips couldn't speak curse words
Yet, it happened that my heart held a grudge
And my brain ran out for bad blood

This hatred seems to be everlasting
A tricycle-riding witch rode over my feet
And my soul that didn't even shed tears
It happened when I'd hardly known of love
Just when I felt at ease about this world

This wound on her back carved in like tattoo
And her guts, it's the only thing to blame
Cause my eyes couldn't stand blood drops
And my wounds didn't seal off like hers
That's when I deeply felt comfort

This story sure does date way back
And this wound over my feet carved in like tattoo
When I was still a tricycle-riding narcissist
And my hands weren't trembling while holding a knife
It all happened, when my heart held a grudge
And my brain ran out for bad blood

©HIDDEN
DEMOISELLE

davydwriter ·
Behind a Tree

⋮

The Grudge

Midnight. Stood in a charity trench coat, synchronicity hiding his treasure, Fred, Churchillian, masculine with amiable greying hair. The turnups of his trousers, laid beside him, made him look taller, laughable, beloved.

People in memoriam, a racing of the heart. Caught with their pants down in a passion rush. Deep high-street headaches. Surprises are not always nice.

Crystal Pebbles...*Dar-Dar*...She presented her cake iced with immoral spirit. Heresy. The fulfilling pop of a champagne cork, dusty thoughts with surprised enormity. Moonlight. The knife's edge glistened. *Surprise Paunchie,* she chuckled.

DavyD

 emm_kay0 ·

The grudge, that would be me

I care not at all, I love too much
Your loss, play the slots, taken in by the gloss,
you know not gold from which is dross, I love too
hard, that lost smile, that mascara smudged,
that broken heart, but that's all a part of the path
we pave, with intention, and inattention, the
asked question.
The paradox of happiness, wanting it more, hold-
ing it less, the laughter assumes the easy answer,
there are no easy answers, sometimes there isn't
one, you pick and choose, both ways you lose
Giving in, giving up, for give and take, you
couldn't make, the hearts stay, and stray they
did, till I say, neither always, nor forever.
Just a story you could forget.
Or tell. Or just remember.
©emm_kay

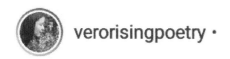 verorisingpoetry ·

Our love was lost in translation,
mixed signals floating in the dense air.
Venom-laced words
said in preemptive haste,
while the beautiful ones
that would've made a difference
were kept buried deep inside,
never to see the light of day.
Eyes filled with Soul,
longing, wishing, pleading
to be acknowledged and heard over
the blaring confusion -
A dead giveaway to the true feelings,
betrayed by angry tones and rigid,

— Vero Rising Poetry.

verorisingpoetry •

defensive bodies
inevitably leading to
inescapable, mile-high stone walls.
Actions that can never be taken back
decorate the Halls of Memory,
a vivid timeline depicting our most
notable failures.
If only we had some type of dictionary
or guide book to make sense of it all.
So much pain and heartbreak,
important moments through the years,
lost and ruined
simply because we spoke different
languages.

– Vero Rising Poetry.

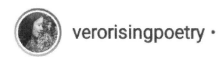 verorisingpoetry ·

Our love became a breeding ground for
ridiculous misunderstandings
that took on a life of their own
and oversaw our demise with glee.
Communication breakdown...
What a damn shame,
how some things just never change.

— Vero Rising Poetry.

secret_words_of_hart ·

The Grudge

Harbouring such bad
feeling
Sending emotions
reeling
For someone's
unforgivable actions
Leads to a resentful
reaction
The grudge...
becomes deep seated
Feeling totally
depleted
Unwilling to forgive
A past continuously
relived

sticksandstonespoet ·
Melbourne, Victoria, Australia

YOU ONLY WANT ME WHEN I'M WASTED
HERE I AM STARVING FOR CRUMBS OF ATTENTION
WASTED AWAY ON YOUR EMPTY PROMISES
BUT YOU DON'T WANT ME NOW YOU'VE TASTED
I'M NO LONGER FORBIDDEN FRUIT
ADD ME TO YOUR COLLECTION
HERE I AM FADING DOWN TO THE BONE
YOU SAID I WAS THE ONLY ONE
AM I SMALL ENOUGH FOR YOU TO LOVE
WATCH ME FADE AWAY RETURN TO DUST
A SHADOW OF WHO I WAS
DAMN STRAIGHT I HOLD A GRUDGE
I DREAM ABOUT FREEDOM
I DREAM ABOUT YOU NOT BREATHING

@sticksandstonespoet

 maria_at_40 ·

A grudge against another,
weighs as heavy as a debt.
A grudge against ourselves,
weighs as heavy as regret.
Debts can be paid,
we can free ourselves of hate.
Regrets can be freed,
if we learn from our mistakes.

 **lismcdermott ·**

Her family were her lifeline her anchor,
Parents who loved her completely, beyond all.
Yet when he came courting, she fell in his thrall
accepting his love, despite her parent's rancour.

They had hoped she would meet anyone other,
than the son of kin they'd fought tooth and nail
and secretly prayed the relationship would fail.
Happier had she fallen for no relations of her mother.

Once they were together and eventually wed,
Her wonderful lover became an absent husband.
Not how she imagined her life, but what he planned.
A merry dance of debauchery with other women he led.

Isabella felt so stupid, how could she so misjudge
her lover? feeling like the victim in an operetta
she recognised, it was a family feud, a true vendetta.
His love was all a lie, nothing more than a grudge.

© Lis McDermott 2021

HOUSE OF PAIN

thedarksideofthephoenix ·

This used to be a happy home,
Before you left me on my own.
You carelessly built for me, a new place to dwell,
And gifted me an eternity of hell,
In this torturous, forsaken house of pain.
You caged my heart inside this house,
Left behind my mind & body to rot.
Locked in turmoil, barricaded inside,
Not one single place that I can hide,
From the many promises that you broke or forgot.
Windows shattered from the force of my screams,
And it seems, as though the walls are moving,
Closing in.
This used to be my safe place, but now I have to face,
Living with your memory,
I avoid sleeping in the bed you shared with me.
It just hurts so much, this house shall never be the same,
I bleed out the venom in my veins,
Staining the sheets, the walls, mixing with my tears,
Breathing life into all of my fears.
If these walls could talk about our love through the years,
They would be crying too...

 r5k.poetry ·

RK.

I'm locked inside,
With nowhere to hide,
Scrambling furiously,
Searching for the key,
I can't stay here,
Living in fear,
I must escape again,
From this house of pain.

poetry_ordeal_solitude_solace_ ·

My heart cries as I see hers cry
And how all the painful things are invisible!
I never once thought this place would've reeked of envy
This place turned into a crashed house of pain
I wish I had the courage to walk a step out or two
Reach out to her
But the past comes in my way, her steps stepping away
She never became the shoulder that I needed
It was me and my unheard screeches
So I keep crying and sobbing inside than reaching out to her
I see her heart cry and just keep watching as it drowns

My heart shatters as I see hers shatter
And how all the misery within remains hidden!
It never once occurred to me I'd belong to where it reeks of rancour
This place has become dead house of misery
I wish I was brave enough to talk a thing or two
Console her
But the past comes in my way, old promises didn't stay
She never approached me in my worst stages
It was me left alone with all blank pages
So I keep breaking and hurting till I can't than talking to her
I see her heart shatter and keep watching as we fade

©HIDDEN DEMOISELLE
(crashed hearts in dead house of pain)

dwainswords ·
London, United Kingdom

⋮

"Walls painted with
my trauma,
picture, picture-frames
with snapshots
of my mistakes"

———————————

Dwain Brown

dwainswords ·
London, United Kingdom

"however, I am
still developing the negatives
leaving the window open
for change,
whilst walking in the right
direction"

Dwain Brown

dwainswords ·
London, United Kingdom

⋮

"I see stains,
on each step
as I climb up the stairs,
in each bedroom
I see,
a child desperate
to be loved
welcome to the
house of pain"

Dwain Brown

 blackwidowpoet ·

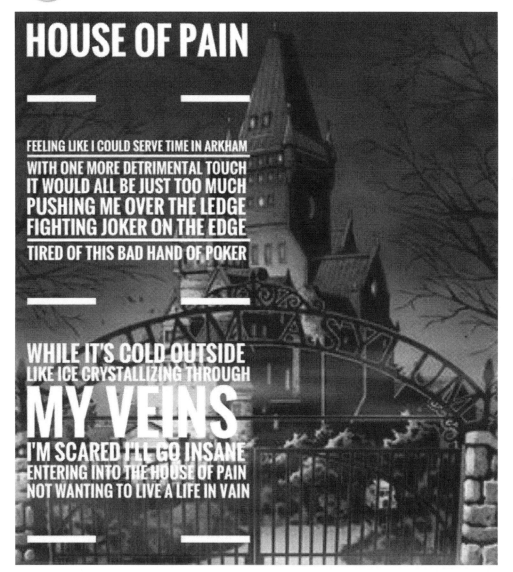

HOUSE OF PAIN

FEELING LIKE I COULD SERVE TIME IN ARKHAM

WITH ONE MORE DETRIMENTAL TOUCH
IT WOULD ALL BE JUST TOO MUCH
PUSHING ME OVER THE LEDGE
FIGHTING JOKER ON THE EDGE

TIRED OF THIS BAD HAND OF POKER

WHILE IT'S COLD OUTSIDE
LIKE ICE CRYSTALLIZING THROUGH
MY VEINS
I'M SCARED I'LL GO INSANE
ENTERING INTO THE HOUSE OF PAIN
NOT WANTING TO LIVE A LIFE IN VAIN

blackwidowpoet ⋮

PAST TRAGEDIES REPLAY IN MY MIND
thinking about what I could do
DIFFERENTLY EVERY TIME
ALTHOUGH I CAN'T PRESS REWIND
hearing giggling sounds of laughter
ALL AROUND
I CRY IN DESPAIR
BECAUSE I DIDN'T GET A HAPPILY EVER AFTER
JUST LIKE HARLEY
I'M STARTING TO LOSE FEELINGS
BUT I'M BREAKING THROUGH GLASS CEILINGS
TRYING NOT TO GET CUT
AVOIDING SINFUL INTERACTIONS
MUCH TO MY SATISFACTION

 blackwidowpoet ·

THIS IS JUST A PREVIEW
OF MY UPCOMING ATTRACTION
ALTHOUGH I SAVED
A LAST DANCE
MAY HAVE ONE MORE
BAD ROMANCE
WHAT REALLY WOULD I GAIN
FROM LIVING IN THIS HOUSE
OF PAIN

COLLABORATION @BLACKWIDOWPOET & NICK ALOYO

writerpoetkim ⋅   ⋮

Sometimes, there are no words...
no words to express
the depth of emotions
raging like a tsunami in your heart.
How wildly they thrash about!
The waves are barely contained within you;
its waters leaking from your eyes,
hot like a jungle river.
They are tears of chaotic waters;
waters filled with hungry piranhas
ready to eat up every part of you.
You are no longer a human,
but a walking house of pain.
How can words express such things?
These misshapen lines
stuck together in various formations.
Sometimes, these emotions are just too strong...
sometimes, there are no words.

@writerpoetkim

ellie.writes2 *

I carry pain like splinters
Beneath my flesh
My heart bleeds a slow death
This melancholy pulse
Barely breathes life into my lungs
Suffocating on nightmares,
Speaking in tongues
Depleting oxygen slightly each day
Yet time stands still, It lingers and stays
Minutes are hours and hours are years
Crying a river of endless tears
Dreams crushed, trust shattered
This fragile heart broken and battered
Seasons change, memories remain cold
Frozen in time, they never get old
A dull ache that doesn't subside
You can run from your past
But you can never hide
E.W.

davydwriter ·

House of Pain

⋮

He's Lost Control

Hailstones always left a moment of transcendence
A strange sense of having no keys, no home
Sometimes he just wanted to sit and pontificate
Realise he didn't really need a crowd for a party

But being spontaneous pulled at his cortex
Left him feeling like a racing car with broken wheels
He wanted to move from the relentless to the sublime
Ditch those boxes filled with poison and heretics

The ice, the ice, stopped him crossing the line

DavyD

crystallotus759 ·   ⋮

HOUSE OF PAIN

I closed the door that leads to heartbreak.
But I forgot that I live in the house of pain.
There is a constant echo for which my ears eagerly await.
In the same house, there are two parallel worlds.
Where I feel you around me but I can't see you or touch.
The bedsheets embroidered with perfumed pixelated memories.
On the dining table, one cup is kept inverted hoping you will
come and pour me some tea.
Your fragrance prevails in our library
all the books are covered with dust for days but your
fingerprints on them are still apparent.
The rocking chair sway at times on its own.
It creaks and makes me cry as well.
I taste you in my tears, for your plausibility to adhere.
Your love was supremely different.
You sacrificed your life for them whom you never met.
Your uniform is hanging on the wall with your bloodstains.
instead of knowing you are already home,
I am waiting for you in this house of pain.

crystallotus

annawriterspage

No Loop

The first time I saw her,
she was playing football with the boys;
Same height, same haircut,
only difference being her voice.
She was shouting instructions
and to my surprise no guy would complain.
But as they grew into young men
she stayed small, forced into a house of pain.
It took her years to learn her worth
and let herself grow too,
meeting new friends and extending family
who just let her do
and be
who she wants
and how she feels free.
She's shining bright on so many days,
sharing her lights in so many ways
with the people who care
and the people who don't.
I'll never hide her again
and make sure that you won't.

- A.Writer

wildernest_poetry

LET NOT YOUR HEART CRY
breaking in a house of pain
THROUGH THE DOOR FLY

free

Elle Wildernest

BASTARD

 debbie_o_bottled_up_feelings ·

YOU CAME UPON MY LIFE
SO UNFORESEEN
I GLADLY LET YOU IN
FOR A TIME
I RELISHED IN YOUR LOVE
WHICH I BELIEVED WHOLEHEARTEDLY
YOU TOOK WHAT YOU WANTED FROM ME
FOR I GAVE IT FREELY
IT'S NOW I SEE
HOW GREEDY YOU WERE
TAKING WHAT YOU WANTED
WITH NO REGARD
WHAT A BASTARD YOU ARE!
TO TAKE MY HEART

DEBBIE O BOTTLED UP FEELINGS

a_c_lawless · Follow

Bastard

I have the longest conversations with the rain
When it pours,
And then the doors
Open and you're ready to snicker and sneer
At the first sign of nerves;
When my body stiffens and voice quivers,
When you ask me questions you know I can't answer.

You're a bastard.

The best part of my day is when you're at work.
I can breathe again.
I'm not on guard waiting for the other shoe to drop.
You flaunt your wealth,
Admire your own stealth
When slipping in and out of rooms just to sneak up on me;
Lying to my friends and family makes me sick.

You're a bastard.

Controlling;
I hate when you're patrolling
The house when I'm in bed.
I hear the creaking of the floor when you walk past several times.
My heart pounds out of my chest imagining the tortures you have planned
For me, and all these things, you see,
The wool was pulled over my eyes.
You're not the man I presumed you'd be.

You're a bastard.

@a_c_lawless

 patriciahelenwriter ·

BASTARD

Dastardly bastard!
Belligerent bloke
thinking himself macho.
What a joke!

His rotten behaviour
(as his ego swells)
isn't appealing.
It only repels!

secret_words_of_hart ·

Ryan Daniel Warner
Do you know i don't swear?
A prompt saying bastard
Now that's really unfair

Yeah i sure damn well could use it
But i'm trying to reframe
Because i have an ex you know
i would surely love to name!

i'm squeezing my mouth shut tight
Trying not to say it
But this is bloody hard you know
As i want to liberate it

Bastard! Bastard! Bastard!
Wow what fun is this?
is it my therapy?
Or are you just taking the piss?

What have you done to me?
Ryan you've made me swear
40 odd years old
And i've always been a square

Led me astray you have
Wait until i tell Emma
Guess what he's taught me?
Your naughty swearing fella

@secret_words_of_hart

beboldtoya
Prompt

*****

stop acting like a *****
when you step to her
like ****
you belong in a ditch
grow some balls
act like a man
stop whining
like a *****
approach her with
respect
she
may
pull
you
out
of
the
ditch without a glitch

@beboldtoya

 elliemorfou

⋮

WHEN LOVE ROTS

Love at first sight
oh Princess! oh my Prince!
always together
like paper and glue
pebbles and waves
a tree and a bird
- for Cupid's sake, like f'ing macaroni and cheese -
and yet love fades
the bowed and arrowed chubby boy leaves
and Hades takes over; time for death.
Gone are the Princess and her Prince.
Where they once stood
you'll find a remnant of their love
a story told whenever someone asks
about the Bastard and the Bitch.

 verorisingpoetry ·

If you think I'm a bitch,
just wait until Karma finds you.
She is ruthless with her justice and
won't hold back like I did.
Vengeful eyes have now set their sights
upon you,
as she adds your name to her
ever-growing hit list of wrath.
If you listen closely,
you can hear her sharpening her claws
already...

*One, two, Karma's coming
for you...*

– Vero Rising Poetry.

 z.b.sayed ·

Bitch

Bitch, is not a swear
It is the attitude you wear

They make you believe, that fighting for yourself is a
crime
So what, if you are called a bitch one too many times.

Some don't like the idea of a woman in lead
You are the answer to this creed.

Crush their insecurities in your style
With daggers in your eyes and lips filled with smiles.

Be proud to be called a bitch
You're the one they're afraid of, you are biggest
badass witch.

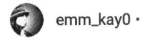 emm_kay0 ·   ⋮

"I CAN'T OCCUPY THIS LITTLE SPACE
IN YOUR HEAD IN YOUR HEART IN YOUR HOME IN
YOUR WORLD IN YOUR LIFE
IT IS ALL OR NOTHING
I WANT EVERYTHING
I AM A BIG GIRL, NOT JUST A GIRL BUT A
PERSON, I AM NOT A BETWEEN-THE- ACTS ACT,
I AM THE WHOLE SHOW, I OWN THE STAGE, I
AM HAPPENING
IN MORE WAYS THAN YOU KNOW
I HAVE A VOICE I HAVE A PLACE
I HAVE STRENGTH MORE THAN ANYONE EVER
KNEW
YOU ARE IN MY HEART, I AM WILLING TO LOVE
YOU, BUT ON MY TERMS."
'BITCH!!' HE SAID.
AND THAT WAS THAT !
EMM_KAY

 patriciahelenwriter ·

BITCH

Blustered to belligerence

Incessantly irked

Toxically tipped

Caustic energy worked

Heralding the...b-i-t-c-h

 m.meanders ·

@jmarie_voe

Bitch is bad
Bitch is thick
Bitch stop playing with me and let me hit
Bitch you make me sick
Bitch was a heart taker
Bitch you finally met your maker
Bitch is hood
Bitch rides this stick good
Bitch go make my food
Bitch who you think you're talking too
I call you bitch because you allow me to
A real woman wouldn't put up with half the shit you do
The constant disrespect the constant back and forth, were so toxic for
each other you too stupid to realize your worth
Bitch drop to your knees
Bitch empty out your account for me
Bitch I'll beat your ass
Bitch I'll put a bullet in your temple
Bitch there's nothing unique about you
Bitch your so predictable
See what I mean, this power I continue to have and you fold every time,
to nieve to recognize how your slowly dying
And Bitch if you ever grew balls and tried to leave... I'll kill myself but
I'll take you with me

STARS AND STRIPES

 penned.piper ·

STARS AND STRIPES, SHE SINGS, A STAR, IN THE SPOT LIGHT. ALL EYES ON THE PROUD GIRL WITH DRESS BLUE AND WHITE, AND RED LIPS THAT KISS THE MICROPHONE IN THE NIGHT AND SHE KNOWS NOT WHAT SHE DOES BUT SHE'S DOING IT RIGHT... SHE SING FEELINGS. SHE SINGS DREAMS, AMERICAN DREAMS, WEBS SPUN FROM LIQUID MELODIES THAT FLOW FROM HER MOUTH LIKE MOUNTAIN SPRINGS TO WATER THE GROUND WHERE YOU SCATTERED YOUR HOPEFUL SEED RED, WHITE, AND BLUE STRINGS, MEANT TO CAPTURE THINGS AND SHE DOESN'T UNDERSTAND WHAT HER SONG MEANS, BUT SHE SINGS, BUT SHE SINGS IN THE LOUNGE WHERE YOU DRINK AND RATTLE THE ICE IN YOUR GLASS OF SWELL THINGS, YOUR GLASS OF CONTENTMENT, YOUR GLASS OF COMPLACENT, YOUR GLASS OF COMPLICIT, YOUR GLASS OF RESENTMENT... HOW COULD YOU BUY IT, THE LIES YOU'VE BEEN TAUGHT, HOW COULD YOU BUY IT, NO BATTLE FOUGHT, THE TIME'S COME NOW, TO FIGHT, NOW THAT YOU SEE, BUT YOU DRINK AND YOU DRINK TILL YOU CAN'T EVEN SPEAK... AND SHE LULLS YOU TO STUPOR, SHE LULLS YOU TO SLEEP AND SHE SINGS AND SHE SINGS AND SHE SINGS YOU A DREAM, AN AMERICAN DREAM, RED, WHITE, AND BLUE, STARS AND STRIPES FOREVER, IF ONLY SHE KNEW, MAYBE SHE'D SING YOU A DIFFERENT TUNE... MAYBE SHE'D SING REVEILLE IN THE MORN AND WAKE YOU TO BATTLE OR WAKE YOU TO MOURN. SING US SOBER DEAR LADY! SING US DRY, TO SOUND MIND, SING THE HANGOVER AWAY IN THE FIRST EARLY LIGHT, LET THIS BE THE DAWNING OF A NEW DAY IN SIGHT... DEAR LADY WITH THE VOICE THAT SANG US THE AMERICAN DREAM, SING US A NEW SONG, STARS, STRIPES AND NEW THINGS. SING US TO SOBRIETY, NO MORE TIME TO WASTE, USE YOU VOICE TO INSPIRE FOR HUMANITIES SAKE, WE DON'T HAVE THE ANSWERS YET BUT AT LEAST WE'RE AWAKE, SINGS US THE MELODIES THAT MAKE THE EARTH SHAKE, SING US BLACK, WHITE, AND BLUE; SING US RED HEARTS THAT BREAK. BRUISE US WITH TRUTH, FROM THE FLAT OF YOUR BLADE, SING US THE SONG THAT UNLOCKS THE CAGE, LADY LIBERTY AT LAST STEP OFF OF YOUR STAGE, LEAD THE CHARGE THROUGH THE STREETS AND IN CHORUS WE'LL RACE... WE'LL SING OF THE STARS AND THE STRIPES OF OUR SKIN, WE'LL SING OUT THE TRUTH AND THEN, ONLY THEN, WHERE THE TRUTH AND THE LIGHT MEET THE STARTS AND THE STRIPS WE'LL UNRAVEL THE WEB THAT YOU SANG IN THE NIGHT AND WE'LL RISE ON SOUNDS OF THE NEW SONG WE SING THE SOUND OF OUR TRUTH SONG SETTING US FREE.
IF ONLY SHE KNEW, SHE'D SING DIFFERENT I THINK
IF ONLY SHE KNEW, I COULD PUT DOWN MY DRINK

-PIPER

poeticbeyond3544 · ⋮

Stars and Stripes to me
Equals to prison bars
And
Constant concussions
Unfair conditions
Mixed with bloodshed
Serving time
Under names and numbers
Not mines except
For the bruises and
Trauma that
Last lifetimes beyond

 patriciahelenwriter

STARS AND STRIPES

With 50 stars and 13 stripes
American flags flutter in the wind.
50 stars showcase national states
13 stripes commemorate colonial origin.

Uncle Sam's red and white and blue
avow strength, purity and vigilance.
This powerful western world nation
strives to evolve in stellar diligence.

COMPLETE FREEDOM

 makinde_kehinde_margret ·

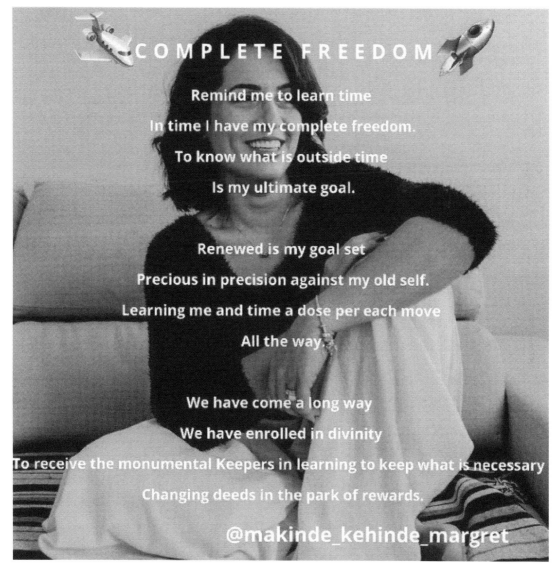

COMPLETE FREEDOM

Remind me to learn time

In time I have my complete freedom.

To know what is outside time

Is my ultimate goal.

Renewed is my goal set

Precious in precision against my old self.

Learning me and time a dose per each move

All the way.

We have come a long way

We have enrolled in divinity

To receive the monumental Keepers in learning to keep what is necessary

Changing deeds in the park of rewards.

@makinde_kehinde_margret

alison.paige ·

When children want to grow up and adults
want to go back.
A mix of longing for simpler times and
wanting a complete freedom we'll never
have.
We think life gets easier with age but it's one
steep hill after another.
Roll down when you reach the top.
Being carefree may not be the same thing as
freedom, but it's a start.

@_alisonpaige_

 verorisingpoetry ·

One day I will leave,
one foot in front of the other...
(Remember – baby steps!)
You, are nothing more than a detour
along the path to Nirvana.
I have aged by your side
and almost went mad too many times
to recount.
Lethargy has set in,
(or maybe it's rigor mortis)
and I cannot run away.
But one day, I will...
You will be struck dumb and consider
it foolish audacity,
that is, until you realize you lost.
What will you do?

— Vero Rising Poetry.

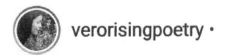 verorisingpoetry ·

Will you go down the rabbit hole and
drown in your tears?
Or is drunk dialing more appealing?
Will you delude yourself into thinking
I am at fault
and yell at all the passersby about the
SLUT/BITCH/CUNT in their midst?
Will you hope and pray and dream
and wish that I die?
Or that I was just a figment of your
imagination?
Will you bite, claw, kick, and consume
the memory of me,
only to shit it out and flush it away?
Will you know that you had the best
and settled for nothing?

– Vero Rising Poetry.

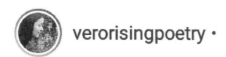 verorisingpoetry •

Perhaps, you will thank the false
prophets for my departure and
find another to replace me.
One day I will leave,
one foot in front of the other
and never look back again.

— Vero Rising Poetry.

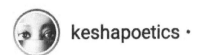 keshapoetics ⋅   ⋮

I nourish my soul
I bake into my beauty
I emerge out, free

@keshapoetics

 **autumnalfyre ·**

COMPLETE FREEDOM

No freedom is as complete
as that found within the borders
of the blank page.
Here, in this quiet realm
I have invented empires
and conjured the souls
of the dead and the impossible
and easily—too easily—I have
silenced them and
made them disappear.
Who but me would stop me?

@autumnalfyre

 joyshribose ·

COMPLETE FREEDOM

I wish to unbraid the tapestry of my mind

That enslaves me from vices of every kind.

To spread my wings and fly

Light and high up in the vast sky...

To paint it with the colours of love and goodness,

Erasing every traces of darkness,

With my warmth to melt the ice barrier

That divides the socio-economic-religious layer.

I pray for a world free from every misery

Where not a single child should go to sleep hungry.

Finally, I seek freedom of the quill

To lay bare my soul at will.

-JOYSHRI BOSE.

 **secretwriter1427** · ⋮

La Liberté Complète (Complete Freedom)

There were too many ways then, keeping us in the trees
but the only way now is forward & through, until we're free
& then I am completely–I am here until I am gone

je suis ici

& just as it does each year for the fall-colored leaves
rustling & tumbling along with the crisp breeze
my hour of departure will inevitably come

mais je suis ici

Summer lingers, avoiding goodbyes, not wanting to leave
until all that is left is emptiness cutting off its strands & strings
as I wistfully wander without concern

et je suis ici

& then amber autumn ambitions drift & slowly freeze
into whittled winter wisdoms that I stretch & store with ease
until spring once again returns

jusqu'à ce que je parte d'ici

-SecretWriter1427

 **annawriterspage** ⋮

Selection Day

Grand lines under heavy clouds
cause a traffic jam in the halls.
They are rushing and buzzing,
bee hive vibes contaminating the area.
It's a busy formation that seems to lack
structure, but it's deceiving.
Any spectator could tell its organization
within one single minute.
There are greeters and security
checking whoever wants to enter,
their faith, perfectly biased, blossoming
into a suspicious glare or questioning stare.
A lady, dressed in a knitted sweater sits,
ticking names off of lists,
later representing all the visitors of this day.
Another one hands out colorful paper, in order
of smallest to largest
with empty places for us to fill.
Other guests play hide and seek
behind improvised prison walls only equipped
with a ball pen.
It takes a few minutes and one plastic container
next to another. Now they're back outside and
complete freedom brushes the faces of
grave misery.

- A.Writer

THE LAMPLIGHTER

alison.paige · ⋮

For all the magic in our hearts,
reality keeps it trapped inside.
The imagination of our youth
dies out with age till the only
fantasy is found in fiction.
We long for tales of royals and
lamplighters to take us away
to another world. To remind us
of the stories we'd spin until
we suddenly stopped.
Well, most of us did.
Life is more entertaining when
your head is in the clouds.

alison.paige

 weatheringthestorm ·

⋮

There are those who hold space for us in the dark

When we can't see our way but they know the path by heart

Who've defeated the ghosts that wouldn't dare face the day

Then turn around and light a lamp for us to find our way

@WeatheringTheStorm

makinde_kehinde_margret ·

🕯️ THE LAMPLIGHTER 🕯️

Most beautiful light I have seen mentions me to the world
Today as concerned with the end
I have been justified by the beginning
From the very start
Words channel me to give in or away
Instant believe is unleashed
Dreaming in seasons
Hours venture chapters of life I wrote
By my deeds, desires and dreams
Today and tomorrow to command symbols
A light I am made by Demiurge to be beautifully lit
Burning bright in perfection perpetually
Have you met the Lamplighter?
He is my Lover in all of Love's infinite dimensions
I a canvas bearing His likeness.

@makinde_kehinde_margret

 **moonlit_odyssey** ·

Swiftly like a dart, he moved
Amidst the peddles of hullabaloo
Chunks of flesh, splinters of spares
Rattling commotion, a daring escape
Barbed wire bulwark beleaguers stigma
A rebel mind, an erupting magma
He, a lamp lighter in the house of pain
Tiny hands prised for a morsel of grain
Cost of emancipation, dearly paid
Penury spurring conscience to degrade

An ungrudging blanket of kindness,
Roofed him from hail!
Droplets of love softly permeated
Holy water purged wretched soul's fate
Erasing bygone scarred torments
Swiveling woes to ebullience...

In the light of the rising sun
An arcadian freedom, an orlay of solace!

moonlit_odyssey

wildernest_poetry ·

⋮

I am the lamplighter
I walk alone through
the city's grey mist
amidst sweeping swirling darkness
as bright light, forthwith,
I bring
whilst upon my heart,
a song I sing
and while though not
exactly a dirge
my soul is smudged and mournful
greased black with
grief and despair
the sort I can not
purge...

🍂Michelle Bell🍂1/3

 wildernest_poetry ·

I could disappear
seep into the
dark corners
and not be missed
for the lonely are forgotten
I could be
a phosphorescent ghost
it would suit
me well, indeed
one might say,
the best, the most
though my light
then, would not
exist ...

Michelle Bell 2/3

wildernest_poetry ·

oh, gleeful irony,
here's the rub,
for my wit will save me,
it's bigger than myself,
you see, as I am the lamplighter,
the light I shed to thee
does shine, as well, in me

Michelle Bell 3/3

debbie_o_bottled_up_feelings ·

Twilight approaches
As the sky turns in hues
Of purples and blues
Battered and ready
To depart into night
The lamplighter always comes
To light the darkness
And show us the way
He walks in solitary obscurity
To illuminate our lives
He walks ahead in Cimmerian shade
And I wonder
Who lights his path?

DEBBIE O BOTTLED UP FEELINGS

 joyshribose •

⋮

THE LAMPLIGHTER

I may not be the tall light house near the ocean

Guiding the ships from destruction,

But striving to ignite the flame of education

Not for the lure of wealth, yet for self satisfaction..

Shaping curious minds was, and still my passion,

Though not a trained full time teacher by profession,

Just a little lamplighter towards a bright destination

Illuminating dark, cobbled alleys of the minds of children.

-JOYSHRI BOSE.

novamarie_poetry · ⋮

Mercy:
to withhold punishment;
and I've been bad.
So here I am
in front of you
on my knees,
asking to be pardoned.
But you say no so firmly,
I can feel it in the back
of my pleading throat.
Unzip my exoneration.
If my tongue begs
for your forgiveness
will you please
teach me a lesson
and vindicate me?

@novamarie_poetry   9/25/2021

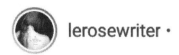 lerosewriter ·

A bite, just one
Laced and ebbing as mercy drowns against the
fault lines that bleed us dry
Immortality waning
Against a cold moon, hanging in a sapphire sky
Who are we, when the prison of flesh crumbles
Scent rising into static voids
At an ungodly hour
When beast meets innocence
In a blood stained sky

Luna Rose

verorisingpoetry ·

Listen motherfucker...
Did you forget about ripping my heart
out?
Did you forget how you left me to bleed
out as you ran?
Did you forget the words you poured on
me like gasoline before you lit a match?
Did you forget how I pled for mercy and
you laughed?
Maybe, you should go see someone for
your memory issues,
because I remember just fine...
And perhaps you should take a little trip
to Oz as well,

– Vero Rising Poetry.

verorisingpoetry ·

and see if you can find yourself
a heart, a brain, and some balls -
since all 3 are so woefully lacking.
As a matter of fact,
why don't you just stay there and leave
me the fuck alone?
You are no longer the place I call Home.

— Vero Rising Poetry.

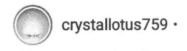 crystallotus759 ·   ⋮

MERCY

Seeking refuge in death
For the grieving soul to set free
from the cage of ribs and flesh.
Is never an option to escape.
Million times you tried
Million times you failed
Yet you rise and fight again
Don't give up upon
hope, trust, and faith.
One who holds the power
Of life and death
destruction and rebirth
One who releases us
from our sins.
Will pour the mercy on us.
Boost your strength
to be used as a channel
by almighty,
to end the crime against
humanity, kindness and love
 The criminals will get destroyed
In their crime hubs.
One day justice will be done.

crystallotus

a_c_lawless · ⋮

Mercy

Bless me Father, for I have sinned
It has been a while since my last confession
Reconciliation is what I seek
I need strength when weak
When nights are bleak
Now I fear it has become an obsession
I will forever bow my head in sorrow
My relationship with God is in need of repair
Can you do that Father?
Fix what I've done,
Reverse time for everyone,
So I don't live in misery and despair?
He came out of nowhere, you know
And as he lay dying, I never showed him mercy
I cannot forgive myself
I pray, pray my soul to keep
Lay hands on me as I weep
What I denied this man, is the very thing I need

@a_c_lawless

 patriciahelenwriter ·

MERCY

When I was a little child
I begged a merciless god
for a shower of sweet mercy
to cleanse of my flawed soul
to rid me of the stain of sin.

Then one day
I was caressed by the wind
and the birds sang to me
while the sun shone warmly
and illuminated the truth
and my soul was light
and I clearly understood
the nature of mercy
and at last I was free.

m.meanders ·

Mercy,
It's not for me
Why don't we sit here,
Aimlessly
Why don't we
Relive the fights
And the nights
And rip ourselves
To pieces tonight

@M.MEANDERS

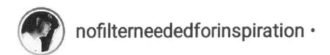 nofilterneededforinspiration ·

Would you listen to my plea?

Can you see the toll?

Even down on blooded knees,

I'm Stuck in my hole,

Could you set me free?

Do you find me droll?

Do you have mercy?

On my damaged soul?

~justluke

@nofilterneededforinspiration

thedarksideofthephoenix ·

Darlin' I want to hear you scream,
Things aren't always what they seem.
Pain or pleasure, why not both together?
I'll place you under my spell forever.
I'll show you no mercy, unless you beg for more,
Tell me what you want, or i'm out of that door.
Reveal to me now, your darkest desires,
No turning back, you've ignited the fire.
Darlin' please, don't hold back any longer,
These ripples of desire just keep getting stronger.
Grant me no mercy, for all of my sins,
Punish me thoroughly, until I give in.
So come with me, let's ride these waves,
One look from you & you know I will cave.
Hands on my hips, pulling me down,
Become lost in my ocean, get ready to drown...

RUMPELSTILTSKIN

 emm_kay0 ·

A walk through the greens to the pub to meet a friend

Can be the end. A deadly game for you are game
for you are a woman a woman is game, and
a game, this walk is your last for you have no
future, no present, your life is past
Rumpelstiltskin has no need of power, wealth and
clout, his knack of creating gold out of straw, but
he is made of it, mud and straw, he can't make a
life new with his magic as a woman can do.
A woman to hold, a woman to empower, a
woman to disembowel, in death in violence
a voice to stifle, the world's conniving silence
Someone to be grateful to him and so take care
of him in return, like children and parents' love
for each other, not a sister, not a mother, not a soul
that would turn from evil.
It's time to spill the truth, the victim is next in
waiting, the perpetrator ready to kill. Again.
©emm_kay

sticksandstonespoet ·
Melbourne, Victoria, Australia

YOU'RE JUST LIKE A FAIRY TALE ..GRIMM
SPARKLING GOLDEN LIES DIPPED IN BLASPHEMY
WHAT TREACHEROUS TALES YOU WEAVE
MY VERY OWN RUMPLESTILTSKIN

@sticksandstonespoet

crystallotus759 ·

RUMPELSTILTSKIN

Rumpelstiltskin giving lessons on not to do things .
The sunrise in the eyes can't be sustained by avarice
Just like the broken glass can't be filled.
Similar way hay straws into gold, you can't spin.
Don't make promises which can't be fulfilled.
Think before speak instead of living with guilt.
Your anger may tear you apart like Rumpelstiltskin
By harbouring rage within yourself, you can't win.
Only you can take windfall at someone's vulnerability
Overconfidence can hand over your soul to the devil.

 patriciahelenwriter ·

A miller tells the king a lie brazenly bold.
He says his daughter spins straw into gold
in his hopes his daughter will become queen
the miller behaves in this manner obscene.

The king demands gold the woman to spin
or his face dire consequences therewithin.
Long- story -short...enter Rumpelstiltskin
with his evil powers gold he easily spins
for the promise of a royal child firstborn
which renders the woman hopelessly forlorn
because not another day alive she'll not see
unless with this unnamed man she agrees.
But it's possible to void this dark covenant
if she speaks his name- not yet in evidence.
The evil man inadvertently his name slips
and when 'Rumpelstiltskin' leaves her lips
the little man renders into two body pieces
and from the covenant she's granted release.

Consider for a moment or two
this could actually happen to you.
Perhaps in a matter not dramatic
but allow me to be most emphatic
that if of the impossible you boast
you risk to lose what you love most.
When with evil you barter once or twice
you set yourself up to pay a steep price!

alison.paige · ⋮

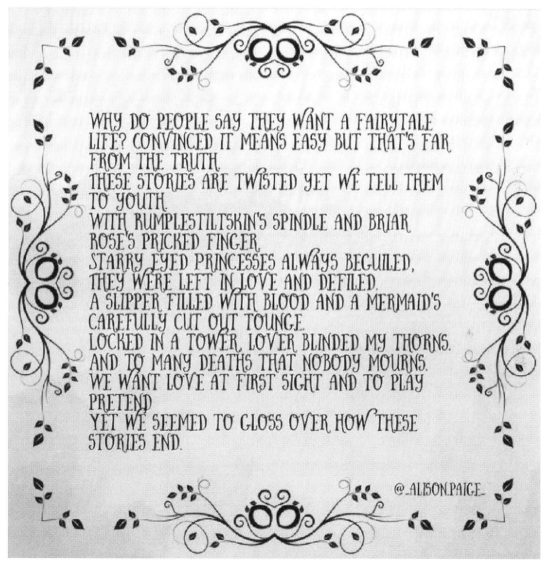

WHY DO PEOPLE SAY THEY WANT A FAIRYTALE
LIFE? CONVINCED IT MEANS EASY BUT THAT'S FAR
FROM THE TRUTH.
THESE STORIES ARE TWISTED YET WE TELL THEM
TO YOUTH.
WITH RUMPLESTILTSKIN'S SPINDLE AND BRIAR
ROSE'S PRICKED FINGER,
STARRY EYED PRINCESSES ALWAYS BEGUILED,
THEY WERE LEFT IN LOVE AND DEFILED.
A SLIPPER FILLED WITH BLOOD AND A MERMAID'S
CAREFULLY CUT OUT TOUNGE.
LOCKED IN A TOWER, LOVER BLINDED MY THORNS.
AND TO MANY DEATHS THAT NOBODY MOURNS.
WE WANT LOVE AT FIRST SIGHT AND TO PLAY
PRETEND
YET WE SEEMED TO GLOSS OVER HOW THESE
STORIES END.

@_ALISON.PAIGE_

LEAD BELLY

alison.paige ·   ⋮

Tea with the Mad Hatter, sometimes the
always late white rabbit.
Our little party every day but one, our
tradition, a habit.
The ticking of the two day off pocket
clock to the drunken singing of the
leadbelly doormouse half asleep in the
teapot.
I celebrate my un-birthday in this
wonder-underland and on my real one I
accept reality as much as I can.

@_alison.paige_

 patriciahelenwriter ·

LEAD BELLY

Huddie William Ledbetter
was a blues and folk superstar
known as the cool Lead Belly
who played a 12-string guitar.

He sang earthy folk and blues tunes-
with his gravelly voice resounding
and throughout American concert halls
his audiences deemed him astounding.

His gift for melodic storytelling
and his accomplished musicianship
make Lead Belly a magical master
who from memory will not slip.

 emm_kay0 ·   ⋮

Goodbye Irene

The autumn sun was pale in the sky, the
evening star about to rise
The porch was dreaming of cotton flowers,
the wicker chairs draped in muslin pale and
white
Her requiem for her lost memories
Held her hand in reprise, the summer birds
had flown, her youth was gone, her reverie
softly calling her soul to fly, she could hear
the lost voice of lead belly crooning in the
pines, her song had forgotten her, it had been
a long time
She had said her goodbyes, and knew her
lined palms caressing her lined face was the
last caress
She sighed just once and closed her eyes.
©emm_kay

 **beboldtoya**

Lead Belly
****

S
T
R
O
N
G
vocals searched
the crowd
accompanied by floating
sounds from his
piano
his
harmonica
binding the souls of folks
like a book
his
words
dressed the crowd with
mental images
of his time behind bars
guilty of
murder
he bonded with
sweaty inmates
as they
clanged their shovels together
digging holes in the scorching sun
Belly sang his way into a pardon
five years later his violent
behavior sent him back to
prison
the saga continues
shifting to
tales of
dirty nappy headed farm boys
and gals
picking cotton
with parched lips
busted toes
lyrics
from his blues
danced with curious
listeners
erupting anger
in their clenched fist
his
prison music
his
slave music
entertainment for some
historical lessons for some
for others 🪦

@beboldtoya

ROAD TRIP

 _alison.paige_ ·

My childhood was a road trip, going
from one place to the next.
I have friends who have never left
the state yet I've slept through
almost all.
When an eight hour drive is a day
trip; too bad I get car sick.
Disney parks every year and a
thousand souvenir shops, I've been
to them all.
Now I want to see the world.
Will you join me?

@_alison.paige_

 z.b.sayed · ⋮

Road Trip

All that noise in the car
We don't know where we are
Holding a map in my hand
I wish this trip was better planned
All we see is an empty road ahead
This road trip is causing a lot of stress
The weather is as hot as the oven
The roads are deserted like, the calm before trouble
One wrong turn and we are lost
I see an old car following us, are we being stalked?
Horror movies are playing back to back in my mind
To top that, the gas tank shows an empty sign
The cell phone batteries are dead.
My poem quickly needs to end
If someone finds my poetry in time
Please come looking for us, we may still be alive.

Z.B. Sayed

 **autumnalfyre** ·

ROAD TRIP

I could pick up and leave on a moment's notice
Drive for days until I reach the ocean
Put on sunglasses and play the music loud
Stop in small towns to avoid the crowds
Stay for a while and see what I find
Let go of worries and free my mind
Some days my wanderlust is quite severe
It seems that anywhere is better than here
I'd travel light; I don't have much to pack
I'm ready to get in the car and never come back

@autumnalfyre

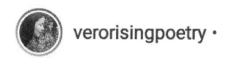 verorisingpoetry ·

Begin listening to those voices within,
they are your personal GPS system
guiding you to happiness and growth.
At times, they may lead you through
some bumpy & admittedly sketchy
moments in life,
but in the end,
you will always arrive
exactly where you need to be.
Remember,
your journey is yours and yours alone.
So, surrender with a smile and
finally trust yourself,
before you wreck yourself.

– Vero Rising Poetry.

 verorisingpoetry ·

Take the back roads and scenic routes
as your soul experiences
a fantastically epic joyride.
Don't forget to make lifelong memories
& take lots of pictures along the way.
One day, you may want to take a trip
down Memory Lane,
looking back at how you got here,
heart bursting with love and pride
at the version of you that took the
chance to be brave.

– Vero Rising Poetry.

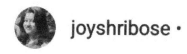 joyshribose ·

       ⋮

ROAD TRIP

A treasure trove of beautiful memories

Of my road trips, etched in my mind's diaries.

Like flipping the pages of a picture book

Every bend of the road offers a new look.

High altitude road trips, laced with adventure

Amidst the snow-clad mountains,with the wave of zephyr

Unlike train journeys, hopping out at an impulse

To soak in the magical ambience of benevolence

Sipping hot tea or coffee

Enjoying local cuisine and culture without any hurry.

Such intangible little pleasures on a road trip

By air or sea route, one has to painfully skip.

                      -JOYSHRI BOSE.

patriciahelenwriter ·

ROAD TRIP

With three little kids
and a mortgage to pay
Mom and Dad work hard
paving a good life's way.

A road trip is a priority.
On an adventure they go
traveling just 200 miles
with a small camper in tow.

There's so much to see
along the winding highway
with stops for hamburgers
and strawberry sundaes.

Who can spot a red VW?
The road trip contest begins-
one that each of the children
is more than eager to win.

And so passes the time
as up the highway they go.
This happy family of five
with a small camper in tow.

 drkeypoints ·

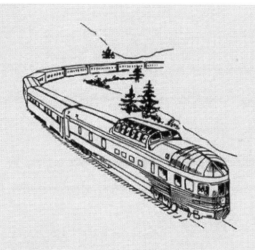

Tattooed rays of sunshine's kiss
Embraced alps parfum on left cheek
Winding road trip of sleepless adventures
Light feather with the world on my shoulder
Sweet spicy fingers,
Our lips traced with honey butter
Moving train and us alone,
My heart with you is happier.

DR.KEYPOINTS

 nicolejadepoetry ·

I'M COMING HOME

Nicole Jade poetry

THROUGH ROLLING PEAKS,
CITY STREETS
AND THOSE WEIRD WINDY ROADS IN BETWEEN
TO SALTY SHORES
WE'VE TRAVELLED BEFORE
AND THE FORESTS WE'VE NEVER SEEN
UP MOUNTAIN PASSES
SCENT OF SWEET MOLASSES
PINNED ON MAPS OF PLACES WE'RE KEEN
TO VISIT ONE DAY
ONCE FATE HAS ITS WAY
BUT RIGHT NOW OUR GRASSES
ARE EQUALLY AS GREEN.

 secretwriter1427 ·

Turn it Around

(after Todd Chavez said)

"You turn yourself around. That's what [the Hokey Pokey is] all about"

Time makes no exception, especially not on this road trip of life; if you make the wrong turn / **you turn yourself around, that's what it's all about** / love yourself like a main character, learn your flaws, live without doubt / A broken glass cannot be filled without its contents seeping through the cracks / but, given time, the cracks can be smoothed over, made somewhat complete / Time may make no exceptions, but that does not make it your enemy / **We fall so that we can learn to pick ourselves up**, to know that we can / so sing along to your own soundtrack, stumble through the notes that are too high / & dance like no one is watching-turn around & shake your booty toward the sky

~SecretWriter1427

harrywritespoems

My dear come walk with me a while, I have so much to say

Let's take a road trip somewhere, to another day

I loved you once, with each fibre of me until the fibres decayed

The stitches of my heart and soul have splintered, torn and frayed

For now time is our divide, one in which we don't grow

Our roads go separate directions, our seeds we do not sow

For you I am grateful, for it is now I know

What it's like to love someone and have to let them go.

BIGGER THAN MYSELF

 joyshribose ·

BIGGER THAN MYSELF

Bigger than myself, is the one above

Under whose will, my head I humbly bow.

I am not a preacher, just a mere observer...

For life itself is a great philosopher.

Human endeavour through technology

Prides himself in shaping his destiny,

But fails to realize in his arrogance

Despite taming disease, time and distance,

Bigger than us mortals, is the divine force...

The writer of our life's script, having the last laugh, of course!

-JOYSHRI BOSE.

 z.b.sayed ·

⋮

Bigger than Myself

A community is bigger than myself, I know
The good parts though, for me are low
A mob mentality sometimes they show
Everyone wants to go with the flow
Thinking for yourself is detrimental
Social approval is always essential
If there is something really bigger than myself, out there
It's the idea of humanity, that as humans, above everything we share
No religious belief can deny that
Unless scriptures have been wrongly interpreted and hijacked
So let acceptance and tolerance guide us
Then no evil, no wickedness will ever incite us.

Z.B. Sayed

 **autumnalfyre** ·

⋮

PARADE BALLOON

I want to create
something bigger than myself,
something to take up more
than my allotted space
and hover like a parade balloon
trailing behind me
even after I'm gone,
something massive for me to point to
and still claim as mine
when it's taken on a life of its own
and snapped its strings
to float along on its own route
wherever the wind leads it

@autumnalfyre

 petren33 ·

I am bigger than myself,
At least my old self,
She has been left on a shelf,
I am no longer really her,
At least not on the outside,
Because deep down we're the same,
That hasn't really changed,
I've always been me,
This person I am right now,
I just couldn't quite always see it,
But now I'm being me,
I have the courage to live as this person,
As me,
I am bigger than my younger self.

@petren33

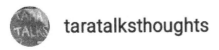 **taratalksthoughts**

I hope to achieve something bigger than myself

I question if it's ego
but I really need to help

Raising awareness on mental health
and on how simple and important consent is

Should be no issue - no is no

Misogyny, harassment and victim shaming

Societies disgusting undercurrents
spread through a persistent hum.. or fizz

Buzzes of boys push you because they like you

Whispers as, for him, she loses her voice

Limiting options - the desire, really to just be yourself

Stripping body autonomy, rights, freedom and choice

 **taratalksthoughts**   ⋮

Pushing into 'nice' boxes and presenting the idea of desire to please

Grooming in, who's to tell us, which way

No choice to walk at night without fear

Without fear of even being believed

The perception that they were 'asking for it'

Dissected, broken down
as misogyny starves and bleeds

I don't know I'm always ready

But tired of how 'complaints' are minimised when received

I'm ashamed to say that I can't always talk

So many fighting oppressive controls

A huge paper ball of ripped up stories

Sobs and 'just another' details in each paper tear or fold

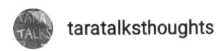 **taratalksthoughts**

Shredding trauma - numb, angry, flat, exhausted

It's an everyday occurrence for many girls and young women

Hurts to think of moments dismissed

Mansplaining, the constant 'not all men' deafening response retorted

No validation

Language matters, rape culture to be lit up in this horrific space

Examined and terminated

School, work, living, renting - needing all within a safe place

The stories that touch us
Each one we hope the last time
Please, this has ended

News a trigger for so many

Collective experiences no longer defended

benjaminsart

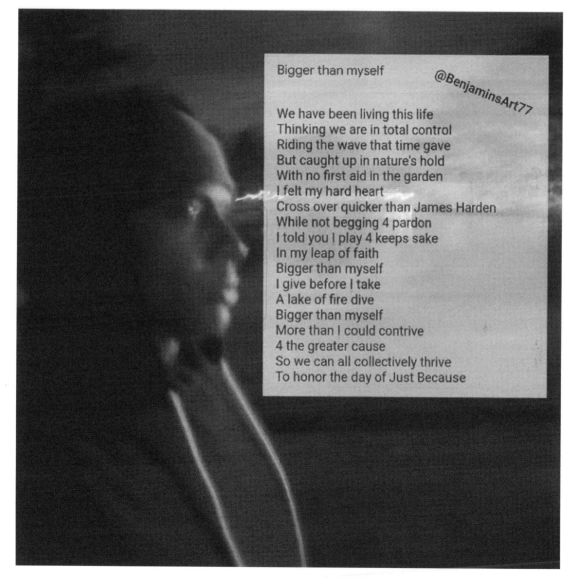

Bigger than myself

@BenjaminsArt77

We have been living this life
Thinking we are in total control
Riding the wave that time gave
But caught up in nature's hold
With no first aid in the garden
I felt my hard heart
Cross over quicker than James Harden
While not begging 4 pardon
I told you I play 4 keeps sake
In my leap of faith
Bigger than myself
I give before I take
A lake of fire dive
Bigger than myself
More than I could contrive
4 the greater cause
So we can all collectively thrive
To honor the day of Just Because

EVAPORATION

 weatheringthestorm ·

The rain comes cascading down
Flattening the flowers
Insects finding cover to cower
Flooding all the edges
Creeping up over curb ledges
Looking like it will never stop

Lightning gives its final strike
The sky slowly lightens
Just as it was looking like night
The rain finally abates
Sun helping it evaporate
The wait was not for naught

@WeatheringTheStorm

ren.d.vous_love ·

Construct,
But do not destruct,
What is beyond human conduct,
When we should not obstruct,
Paths that Mother Nature has instruct,
Upon us,
Mere souls only here for a moment,
Yet claiming everything as a token,
Of what we are entitled,
Just because we are created,
To inhabit this home,
Like it is our own,
Only forgetting
This place is on loan,
In the end we must return,
To its originator,
But will it be in a state too dire,
Or will we return it in its full attire?

-Rendezvous Love-

 autumnalfyre ·   ⋮

Evaporation of Memory

I filled my childhood diary
With dreams of how I wanted things to be
All the words I poured onto the page
At that impressionable young age
Glossed over the big real-life events
Like moving away or grandparents' deaths
There wasn't anything I wanted to recall
Now it's like I wasn't there at all

@autumnalfyre

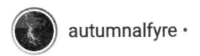 **autumnalfyre ·**

⋮

Because the memories have evaporated
From past times I'm separated
By a decade or two of disillusionment
Mixed with enthusiasm and artistic intent
I was waiting for my life to start
When I should have just taken part
Instead of jotting notes and random thoughts
On the songs I liked and the shows I saw
I've lost memory of my experience
Sometimes I wonder, what's the difference?

@autumnalfyre

sticksandstonespoet ·
Melbourne, Victoria, Australia

AM I TOO LATE
DID I MISS THE STARTING GATE
PERHAPS THE MOMENTS GONE
I'M JUST REOPENING SCARS
I SHOULD FORGET AND BURY
I CAN'T GO BACK
REVERSE THE SITUATION
I'M HERE AGAIN ALL ALONE
WISHING ON DEAD STARS
WITNESSING MY HOPES EVAPORATION

@sticksandstonespoet
©dmccarthy

 writerpoetkim ·

Evaporation

What happens to tears
once they evaporate?
The feelings too strong
to hold in our bodies,
releasing themselves through our eyes.
Do they return to the ether,
and follow us the rest of our days?
Do they float up into the heavens,
joining their brethren from other souls
in the throws of emotion,
and return to the earth through rainclouds?
Maybe they disappear into another dimension;
a dimension where water runs free,
and they live the rest of their existence
in wild adventure.
I wonder what happens to evaporated tears;
I hope it is a future they crave.

@writerpoetkim

 secretwriter1427 · ⋮

Evaporation

I am drowning in darkness, until suddenly I am not-

it's as if the darkness rapidly evaporates, leaving just me

my tears are now frozen reminiscences of inescapability

& then suddenly I can see, I am no longer blind

suddenly this life feels weightlessly bright, light & just fine

~SecretWriter1427

 **bethsaidso**
Texas

UNRAVEL.....
YOU UNRAVEL YOURSELF, UNTIL
THERE'S NOTHING ELSE TO
UNTWINE.
HAVE MERCY(13.)....LATELY, IT'S
BEEN SUCH A BIND BETWEEN
LETTING GO, AND CONTINUE WITH
THE FLOW, OF EVERYDAY LIFE, IT
SLOWLY TARES DEEP INTO THE
POCKETS OF MY SOUL. WIFELY
DUTIES THAT I HELD
RESPONSIBILITY TO,
AREN'T MINE IN THIS PRESENT
TIME, THE INTIMACY THAT WAS
LIKE A FINE WINE, IT GETS
BETTER AND BETTER OVER TIME.
IT'S BIGGER THAN MYSELF(17.)
NOTHING I COULD OF DONE TO
PREVENT THE FALL, PROMISED
YOUR CALL, BUT I'M LEFT
TALKING TO THE WALL, WITNESS
THE EVAPORATION(18.) OF YOUR
BODY, BUT YOUR PRESENCE
STILL LINGERS NEAR,
UNWANTED, LIKE AN INSECT
STUCK IN THE SPIDER'S WEBB,
THE ANNOYANCE CONTINUES AS
MY PATIENCE GROWS THIN, IT
MUST BE A SIN TO HOLD AN
IMMENSE TURMOIL WITHIN ONE'S
ENTIRE EXISTENCE...
#BETHSAIDSO

werdsmith5121 ·

Deciduous

- Werdsmith

I let it go, let it fall from my core. Gave it its due
then showed it the door. I dropped all remnants
and anything that was evident. For me the nude
was cleansing. For the loss a rude blessing.

Water is accepted because it's clear, I can see
through with no fear. A rugged exterior keeps
approaches inferior, even the axe hesitates. The
reach of my limbs fends off envious grins, now
that I've shed the weight.

There's a point of no return when the sun no
longer burns. The dead have learned the
importance of discern. Descending slowly onto
cold ground, it remains that way until planets
come back around.

HOLY WATER

 lerosewriter ·

Steep me in holy water
Until I drown
Until my lungs are mermaid graves
And the church of my breast aches with
stagnating solitude
Crown me, in crevices of flower brigades
Open and close upon hymns of sepia yesterday's
Lost particles
Wrapped in chains
Not letting me go

Luna Rose

thedarksideofthephoenix ·

There is no coming back from this hell, this obliteration,
No effective potion to help mend, only able to provide some sedation.
You've never felt the way I do, how could you? When you refuse to feel anything real.
But you should know yourself, cursed wounds never heal.
The heart rending, world ending,
Tearing of one's soul.
The agonising torment of no longer feeling whole.
Mind splitting, hard hitting, punch to the gut, loss of control.
So please stop trying to convince yourself, that I will be alright,
What part of 'you have utterly & completely broken me, twice',
Don't you get?
Did you forget, that your demons became mine?
YOU planted these monsters into my mind.
And your demons are so strong, they drink holy water like a fine wine,
Salivating as they dine.
Feasting on my actualized fears,
Basted in self-loathing & seasoned with grief flavoured tears...

 crystallotus759 ·   ⋮

HOLY WATER

When I am taking my last breath on my death bed,
don't put me on ventilator, don't feed injections or tablets.
With words of grace and prayers prepare me for my divine
encounter.
Cleanse me physically and spiritually with holy water.
When I am about to begin my final journey.
Feed me a spoon of sacred water and a leaf of tulsi.
After my death for my liberation immerse my mortal remains
into the sacred river Ganga from the Himalayan glaciers
which flows down to the earth.
For salvation, to be retreated, to be nurtured, before rebirth.

crystallotus

kindle.downs ·

And what is September but a series of little deaths

The leaves have begun their descent
Tinged green with summer envy
The milk bottle stars peek fearfully
Over the back of the blood moon
A red heart once waxing
Yet the harvest is upon us
Take the last of this fields bounty
Ripe fruit and grain
Store what comforts you
I will rest a while in fallow
Amongst the rotting things
Sprinkle me in holy water
Pray for this malady to pass

— Linda Downs

 writerpoetkim ·

Holy Water

These tears are holy water,
birthed from the triumphant end,
of one of my life's greatest hero's journeys.
The sacrifices, the pain, the isolation,
all worth their cost in the end.
I had a vision,
and I committed to it.
Even when the naysayers laughed at me,
disregarding my dreams,
I pressed on.
I held on to my inner truth,
and I succeeded.
These tears are of precious waters,
the river of my very heart.
I stand here, victorious.
I am now ready,
for the adventure,
of my next hero's journey.

@writerpoetkim

a_c_lawless ⋅

Holy Water

Be it through sinners or saints,
Do what the good Lord taught her.
Let it burn going down
As she drinks the Holy Water.
Cleanse her from the inside out,
Until not a drop is left.
What power this liquid inside her be,
To flush out the pockets where her demons are kept.

@a_c_lawless

 ellie.writes2 ·

⋮

Your touch is my holy water
My only salvation
I have a confession
Love is my religion
I'm on my knees praying
Lips parting, hips swaying
Our bodies are yearning
To be saved from this aching
Let us worship this insatiable desire
Our passion will set this alter on fire
E.W.

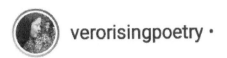 verorisingpoetry ·

You have me stressed to the max and completely
distressed.
I'm utterly depressed and repressed,
feeling thoroughly unclean and insanely
obsessed...
I wouldn't be surprised if you nonchalantly
confessed,
that you had me magically possessed in order to
infest me with demons in cruel, infantile jest.
In desperate need of absolute purification
to stop this never-ending unrest.
Currently on a quest to procure gallons of holy
water and amass ancient prayers that are
divinely blessed.
I fear the only way to expel you from my soul is
with the help of a powerful, self-professed
exorcist.
One with a lifetime of experience in vanquishing
a most unwanted guest,
intent on destroying me at your selfish behest.

— Vero Rising Poetry.

 werdsmith5121 ·

⋮

Pouring Pain
- Werdsmith

The healing hands of art
mends the torn apart,
scars are reminders.
Some never look and thus
remain shook, burdened
with blinders. Whatever
your art may be, music,
painting or poetry just to
name a few. Let the
creative side ease your
mind and pour the pain
right out of you.

TRUTHSEEKER

 emm_kay0 ·

⋮

You may ask

I may not know, the chances are that I do not
know, for I traverse far and wide, to seek all
that eludes me
I may ask, you may not know, but we can
gather together the seeds of words scattered
through the sands of time
Believe me, it stares you in face, yet so hard
to find, you are a truth seeker too, I see it in
your eyes
Walk with me a while
Let's look at the world with new eyes, without
rancour, without rose colored glasses, without
ego, without vanity
The acorns and grasses, one that is hidden,
one that hides
Sift the truth from the lies
A seeking that never dies
A quest. A journey. Within.
©emm_kay

elliemorfou ·

ADVICE FOR TRUTHSEEKERS

Hands seldom lie
about age, stress, ambition,
occupation, sun exposure, marital status,
determination, cleaning habits or health conditions.

A status marker in their own right.

Truthseeker,
time to waive question marks!
Ask for a high-five, handshake, or hand-kissing instead;
witness the truth unfold before your eyes.

The truth.

A truth is only masked by gloves
must-have accessory of thieves, doctors and princesses;
should I explain why?

@ELLIEMORFOU

 noraravenspeaks ·

A truthseeker sees beyond the written word

Become a justice warrior holding the sword

Of authenticity that cuts through fabricated lies

A beacon striking darkness with golden light

In a world of blindness become the eyes

Of honesty, lending the ignorant your sight

Become love, become light

Truthseeker
-Nora Raven

life_begets_here *Reincarnation of a zestful damsel/ From the Graveyard //*

I slept with a daffodil beside my head and woke up next day in
a graveyard.
Crimson chrysanthemums weeping hard,
For it were the diamond studded dreams,
Unaccomplished, owing to the crystal desire enigma,
Longing for glances of pleasure.
Nevertheless, that wasn't shuttered by the swirling winds,
Instead that falling was for you,
Oh yes, my own self,
Absolutely crisp in the fall,
To reiterate the rumbling cupboards that always try to shut me,
My prowess, my dexterity and the grace I exhibit;
Perhaps, a lot of it was to numb the truth seeker in me.
This graveyard was indeed a distinct rudimentary form
For my puissant reincarnation,
 to make mine,
A love I craved,
The love of triumph and contentment which I'm meritorious of,
Erupting to make my novel self a bodacious star,
A chestnut that shall shine like a sun,
Burnt and now, coruscating with venturous beams of rays,
Also, illuminating the lives of the needy.
Again, I shall now regard this graveyard
As a metaphor for delineating my eloquent self,
Not dainty anymore, but brisk and sassy.
✍ *Divya R Reddy*

kindle.downs ·

⋮

She is falling
Lipstick smudge
Against his tattoo crease
Tender touch
Turned feral yearning

Splinters lay bleeding
Living in the mirror world
Illusions shattered
Lamb's for slaughter bleating

Perfume desire rising
Truth seekers
Archway to the house of pain
Lights illuminating

Guiding, welcoming them all the way home

— Linda Downs

secret_words_of_hart ·

What is a truth seeker?
I wasn't exactly sure
But now I think I am one
Because I like to keep
truths pure

If I don't believe allegations
To be completely true
Please rest assured
I won't condemn you

I totally disagree
In wrongful slanderous facts
To be honest
I want no part in that

You could say
I'm a peace keeper
Against wrongful blame
I don't believe untruths
Should go against your name

I've been in these positions
Where tables turned on me
When honesty was all I gave
And slander set on me

So you could say
I'm a truth keeper
And hate to tell a lie
Lies don't sit well with me
Only truths I do comply

@secret_words_of_hart

 secretwriter1427 · ⋮

Insta vs. Reality

A scroll through Instagram's social media feed-
as I nonchalantly window shop for a bit of vicarious living-
plunges me into a spiral of what if's, of missed opportunities
until I remember that my life is the only one I ought to be living

The edited body forms a part of your narrative
while the real one softly exists separate & apart
As you curate, filter & display your regurgitated reality,
are they invisibly saturated, all your phantom insecurities?
or does the piranha of photoshop tear them apart?

From the comfort of their own homes
& bold behind the protection of their screens,
myopic misinformation mutates & is spread by
truth-seekers, bullies & the whole lot in-between

The sour aftertaste of imagining another life lingers,
the mindfuck of social media still stays the same
& while we opt to remain amongst the living
the glass-hearted ghosts continue to play their game

~SecretWriter1427

 writerpoetkim ·

Truthseeker

I am a truthseeker.
I read and research,
I stumble and fall,
down many-a rabbithole.
I want to learn,
I want to grow,
and it is the truth
that will help me do so.
I want to know
all this world has to offer;
my curiosity can never be satiated!
This is my life
as a truthseeker.
Precious truth come my way!

@writerpoetkim

truth.seahorse ·

She shines a laser light
on deception, distortion, duplicity;
seeks out those small innocuous lies,
apparently incongruous details.
Unpicks the carefully constructed
fabric of falsehood.
Her incisive intuition cuts through
the fine filigree of artifice
designed to ensnare and entrap.
Wise to his wily ways,
she will not be constrained or contained.
His masterfully Machiavellian attempts
at manipulation are transparent
as she directs her truth seeking gaze
at the dark depths of his deceit.

@truth.seahorse

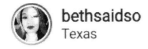

bethsaidso
Texas

⋮

Semicolon

I decided to stay, long ago. I made
that choice despite the short coming
possibilities my future held, I made a
choice for myself, To stand tall as
The Justice Warrior (21.),that no
matter how dark it got inside, I
would always prevail a light that No
one could ever burn out. The light I
speak of isn't identified from one
man , it isn't defined as a Noun,
nothing but a description of Faith
and knowing my place. The toggle
between the evil that lingers from
his beastly characteristics. However.
The knowing, I......did not die!!!! I did
not fade..... I will continue as a
semicolon, in representation of
merely a rest/ break in a sentence,
that leads to a paragraph that
eventually forms into a book that is
left behind for generations to
experience and learn from my
mistakes, short comings and life
lesson about humanity. May they be
as much as a TRUTH SEEKER
(20.) as my mother has instilled in
me.
Sprinkle Holy Water(19.) on every
inch of my existence including things
I touch so it can be as pure and soft
spoken as I wish to be, reflect my
energy to be received as peaceful,
humble, lovingly, as it should
be...Because I'm here to stay, and
choose Life...and to never end it;
#bethsaidso

michellejschoultz ⋮

TRUTH SEEKER

Take a look inside yourself,
delve deep into your being.
Embark on a transformative quest
to discover the meaning of life.

Be a truth seeker;
persist in your open-mindedness,
remain receptive to inevitable changes.

Be a soul searcher;
embrace your unique weirdness,
so you can find your authentic tribe.

Therein, no doubt, you'll realise
all the power you have within:
your truth will emanate,
the love you crave will be in abundance
and your happiness will abound.

~ Michelle J Schoultz

beboldtoya
Truth Hurts

⋮

TruthSEEKER
****

love is truth
truth is love
truth is light
seeking a path that leads to
honesty
starts within the walls of you
disrupting the fragments of
untruths you've told self
S
E
L
F
deserves to know the truth
about the untruths
conditioned to play the
perpetual game
of
L
I
E
S

pretending
to be what you are not
to please society
folks around you
stuck in a world of selfishness
distracted by evil
confined to the dark
S
H
E
confronted her ugly lies
shattered lies
fell like a broken mirror
uncovering the painful
truths
with tears in her eyes
she vowed to stay in the light
away from her bulletproof
L
I
E
S

@beboldtoya

@jmarie_voe

TRUTH SEEKER

TRUTH SEEKER
FEELING SICK
UNEASY FILLING IN THE PIT
EATING FEARS THAT DIGEST INTO MY DIGESTIVE OVERTHINKING SYSTEM
THIS LOVE FEELS LIKE PAIN
THIS LOVE DRIVES ME INSANE
SLEEPING IN THE RAIN
I'M ON THE ROAD FOLLOWING MY MAP, LISTENING THAT MELANCHOLIC
MELODY
TRYING TO FIND THE TRUTH OF WHAT KEEPS ME UP AT NIGHT
ARE YOU WITH HER, WISHING IT WAS ME?
ARE YOU TOUCHING HER, BECAUSE I CAN'T HELP BUT GET THAT FEELING?
MY HEAD THROBS TOO WHERE IT FEELS LIKE IT'LL EXPLODE
MY HEART BEATS SO FAST AND MY BODY OVERHEATS
OVERWHELMED BY THE THOUGHTS OF WHAT YOUR DOING
I HAD TO START MY JOURNEY OF THE TRUTH
IT'S WHAT I TRULY SEEK.
EVENING THOUGH PLAYING THIS DETECTIVE ROLL SEEMS NECESSARY
IT MAKES ME LOW-KEY CRAZY

JUSTICE WARRIOR

patriciahelenwriter · ⋮

JUSTICE WARRIOR

Justice warrior
values democracy.
Justice warrior
respects human rights.
Justice warrior
wards off autocracy.
Justice warrior
wears armor of light.

Justice warrior
works relentlessly.
Justice warrior
levels the field.
Justice warrior
is not ego-driven.
Justice warrior
with fairness -her shield.

life_begets_here *Caressing until forever* / ***The webs we weave*** ✦

Swirling wind that has always been blustering,
Endorses, unequivocally, the intense form of arachnophobia,
That clears off our most puissant visions to retain the WEBS
WE HAD WOVEN,
That resemble our deep longing to stay United;
Our caressing notion to stay back,
With each other, until our last breathe;
To do away with the inane grudges of life, by all means.
In turn, this pigments the tawny twilight sky with tints of
heartbreaks, making it much more murky;
Nevertheless, emancipation of the malicious misconceptions
seek to reside in that process,
Easing our goal to stay together;
Portraying our solves as justice warriors thriving for promoting
VASUDHAIVA KUTUMBA,
That the Universe is one family,
That shall always ascertain the strongest bond
That we, as fellow spiders weave the webs of empathy, solace
and serenity,
And utmost care for each other.
Expunging the grave circumstance of arachnophobia, the fear
of us, which was elsewhere conveyed as the doer of disunity.

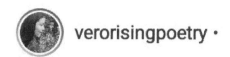 verorisingpoetry ·

I don't want to be saved...
I want to create a life filled with peace
and love.
A life that doesn't rob me of my sleep
or sanity.
A life where I can be myself,
exploring and creating freely.
Where I can be enthralled by all the
beauty around me and can be present
in the moment.
I want a life I don't want to run away
from in order to protect my mental
health or my gentle heart.
A life where I can express myself
without fear.

— Vero Rising Poetry.

 verorisingpoetry ·

A life where I can be appreciated and not scorned.
I want a life where I'm free to dream without ruffling feathers or having to tiptoe on eggshell-lined floors.
I want a life where I can heal others and change the damn world.
I want to love too much, feel too much, and think too much without reproach.
I don't need a savior donned in polished armor, no...
I need a change of scenery where
I can grow and evolve away
from the people and things I need to

— Vero Rising Poetry.

 verorisingpoetry ·

be "saved" from.
I refuse to give up on my vision of
personal utopia.
I don't ask for much -
Just a life conducive to the happiness
that is our birthright.
I don't need to be rescued...
I have my own badass Excalibur
ready to slay monsters,
I just need to gather the courage
to start using it,
once and for all.

— Vero Rising Poetry.

GENGHIS KHAN

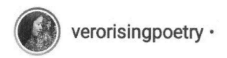 verorisingpoetry ·

Bloodthirsty warrior intent on battle,
demanding others bend the knee and submit like chattel.
Seeing the world as something to conquer,
as you slay those who rebel and call you a ruthless monster.
Heart set on creating a legacy through growing your empire,
you happily set fire to all you can't forcefully acquire.
You don't give a damn about who you destroy on your mad rise to power,
leading you to greedily devour all those who won't cower.
Modeling yourself after the great Genghis Khan,
with brutal brilliance you manipulate people,
as if they were nothing more than a mindless pawn.
A need to be seen and a soul full of greed,
forces you to savagely smite all those who stand in
the way of you becoming a legendary tyrannical icon.
You truly believe you have the divine right to lead,
with every abhorrent and calculated misdeed.

— Vero Rising Poetry.

 patriciahelenwriter •

GENGHIS KHAN

(WHAT I DIDN'T KNOW)

History remembers Genghis Khan
as a fierce and mighty Mongol force
the ruthless 'rags to riches' conqueror
a patriarch and for millions -the source.
Yes...geneticists' research has confirmed
that at least 16 million are descendents
of the tyrant with six Mongolian wives
and 500 young concubine dependents.

sticksandstonespoet ·
Melbourne, Victoria, Australia

I HEARD THE NEWS TODAY
THAT I WOULD NEVER SEE YOUR FACE AGAIN
NOW YOU NEVER TOLD THE TRUTH
AND YOU NEVER KEPT YOUR PROMISES
BUT NOW YOUR FINALLY COMING THROUGH
I GOT PEOPLE OFFERING CONDOLENCES
SORRY FOR YOUR LOSS IT DON'T MAKE SENSE TO ME
LIFE GOES ON WITHOUT YOU LITERALLY
YOU MADE MY LIFE A MISERY
SO TELL MY WHY I'M NOT ALLOWED TO CRY , LITTLE
HAPPY TEARS
INFACT I CAN'T LIE I NEVER FELT SO ALIVE
I ADMIT IT WAS A SHOCK AT FIRST
WHEN I HEARD YOU KICKED THE BUCKET
I NEVER WISHED IT YOUR WAY BUT FUCK IT I CAN'T LIE
TO BE HONEST I'LL BE SLEEPING BETTER TONIGHT
GHENGHIS IS DEAD ..GHENGHIS IS DEAD ON NEW
YEAR'S DAY !!

@sticksandstonespoet
©dmccarthy

FRUIT OF THE WOMB

joyshribose ·

FRUIT OF THE WOMB

Every birth

Is a miracle on earth,

But deprived of the fruit of the womb

Yearning for years for a flower to bloom,

Life slipped by, swallowing every salty tear

In vain trying to conceal from hubby dear.

Where doctors of the earth too failed

Until a miracle from the divine was ordained.

Blessed with the fruit of the womb years ago,

Life no longer loomed like a dark shadow....

Instead like the multi-coloured hues of rainbows

It taught: Nothing remains forever, not even sorrows.

-JOYSHRI BOSE.

novamarie_poetry ·

How do I
tell my mother,
that the fruit
of her womb
has gone rotten?

@novamarie_poetry   9/25/2021

 lerosewriter ·

Settle your heart against the hummingbirds
death
And unfurl your sleep into lungs, petal bound
Ropes of liquorice
Cannot hold this love I have within my acidity

Let it all fall, for tomorrow will be gained in my
blood
Fruit of the womb
Dissolving into rivers that no net can wash free
Angels breath
Warming over an open fire
As autumnal lungs remember what the earth
cradles
A buried egg
Not forced deep enough
To shield me from its memory

An egg softly turning black
And a tear stuck in my dying breast
As one day I'll remember to lay myself
Over the memory of you

Luna Rose

 patriciahelenwriter ·   ⋮

FRUIT OF THE WOMB

As a little child I prayed
"Hail Mary, full of grace"
pressed palms to heaven
sheen on my innocent face.

"...fruit of the womb..."
was part of that prayer
but of the words' meaning
I was not fully aware.

Years upon years later
these words bore relevance.
When I carried a life within
meaning was made evident.

The sacred fruit of my womb
was indeed a gift of grace
and like Mary of my prayers
love flooded my heart space.

 dwainswords · ⋮

"Welcome to Iceland
where we walk on
thin ice, skating around
cold hearts, with frozen morals
snowed under an avalanche
of economic oppression"

———————————————

Dwain Brown

BUTTERFLY EFFECT

poeticbeyond3544 ·   ⋮

Butterfly effect
From a caterpillar's
Crawl
On urban concrete
To overlooking
The city's skylines
Knowing
No ceilings at all

 lerosewriter

He wakes, ruffling oceans with his senses
Tempestuous sanctity, twisted in his sheets;
Sweet depravity,
An echo of a harp played
Formations of a pelvis; mute
He bends
His torso fragmenting into discarded pools
A soul aflame;
He's my muse
A puppet; strings loose
Half a world away..

Stars between us
His pyre ignites
His heart unsheathes breathless delight;
Underneath
My distant core
Unsettling;
Panic button depressed
His need flexed
Convexing..
The butterfly effect;

Passive madness
Drug disintegration
His scented lava, secreting
Slipping through fingertips bound in despair
An open spirit
A friction need so bare..
One held exhale
As his neck muscles twist
Paralytic surrender
He's a void;
Dispelled of dark air

Luna Rose

 noraravenspeaks ·

Since you touched my life

Things have never been the same

It's the butterfly effect

Pieces falling down like a domino game

It's been one disaster after another

Red cape has failed to rescue me

Foundations ripping quicker than I can fix them

And everything's tearing apart at the seams

Butterfly effect
-Nora Raven

joyshribose •   ⋮

BUTTERFLY EFFECT/ DEEP LONGING

A matter of pure serendipity

My deep longing turned into reality.

Just as a tiny pebble dropped in water

Spreads ripples far and long after;

My words unfurled here in my nest

Striving to create the butterfly effect...

My voice through these amazing anthologies

With the delicate wings of poetry reached overseas.

Some inked in nostalgia

Some musings about my country India

Overall spreading universal love, faith and hope

As far as the other end of the globe.

-JOYSHRI BOSE.

onceapterousbutterfly ·

I cocooned long enough,
in loathing & yet was never free,

Perhaps self love is like sunshine,
upon scales of a wing, invisible,

until light allows an observer to see,
beauty, unburdened by opinions,

We fly with our own wing's,
believing & being yourself,
the only, butterfly effect you need;

By Carolina Troy

 secretwriter1427 ·

Butterfly
Effect

~Secret
Writer
1427

a [**Butterfly** (flaps it's wings amidst the chaos
on one side of the world creating ripples
whose waves might unpredictably affect
one thing after another after another until
the chaos on the other side of the world
experiences their) **effect**]

twirlingtyphoon_01 ·

Butterfly

I wish I wrote the way I thought,

spilling some ink my words get caught.

People aren't homes, some say,

Inner child dwelled in me, once gay.

Someday seeking to rewrite the stars,

I fancied shading my scorched scars.

twirlingtyphoon_01 ·

Astonishingly ashamed of the wildflower,

I lost myself to the medal of horror.

Settling in an allure of darkness,

my butterfly withered warily in sadness.

Leaving a trail, towering over my defences,

fallen angel disappeared in dauntless despairs.

Stranded in seconds the symphony was wrecked,

humming heart to the loss of the only friend.

twirlingtyphoon_01 ·

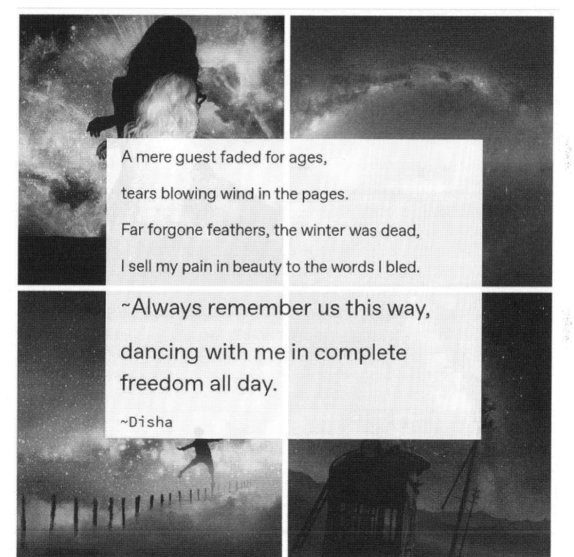

A mere guest faded for ages,

tears blowing wind in the pages.

Far forgone feathers, the winter was dead,

I sell my pain in beauty to the words I bled.

~Always remember us this way,

dancing with me in complete freedom all day.

~Disha

ela.solar
Poem

"butterfly effect"

In the never ending twilight
covered with the starless night
silent and gloomy
cold souls ripple on
the lifeless swamp.
Caught in the mouldy air,
time itself is motionless
only eerie fog creeps around.
A choking stillness
dripping unbearably slow
drop by drop...
But then
a smile
flashes and dies like a spark.
And back to dark silence again...
Another spark flashes
a whisper of laugher
Then another one
And another one
Soon a swirl of light breaks through
the gloomy surface,
infusing cold souls with warmth.
One by one, they start to dance
in the golden tornado
rising to the sky.
Oenomel sunlight
illuminates caliginous sky

by Ela Solar

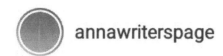 annawriterspage

Waiting for better days

as if rain drops on lanterns

caused all misery.

When those jealousy eruptions on

weekends are the reason

a butterfly effect runs through

this damned relationship.

You are the same in every season

finale, meaning bad endings.

And I won't know until I leave

what role am I playing?

- A.Writer

beboldtoya
Imagination

⋮

Imagination
****

his mind traced the silhouette
of my curves
lingered in the
arch of my lips
sipping
JS RUM PUNCH
I felt his touch
I closed my eyes
followed my imagination
towards the
sensual flames of
Velvet Hammer Cocktail
from
SCENTED BY STEPH
I welcomed the
BUTTERFLY
E
F
F
E
C
T
racing up and down my
WELLNESS YONI
with agility
the tips of my fingers tingled
as
I unwrapped my legs
loosened my thoughts

I

touched myself
and
allowed myself to breathe in rhythms
calculating the rise and fall
in my chest
I
released my inhibition
allowing her to float
I probed farther
entering uncharted territory
at my own risk
with black Diamond
#WETKITTY
purring like a cat
to the
motions of
Max Thrusting his Love Machine
legs extended
screams escaped
my paired lips
dripping I sipped
the
S
P
I
L
L
S
of JS Mango Rum Punch

@beboldtoya

wildernest_poetry
Autumn Woods

autumn leaves falling
monarchs fluttering
the butterfly effect

HE WHO LAUGHS LOUDEST

my.josie ·
Hobart, Tasmania

Don't put me in a place where I need to
accept your apologies...
Spare me the time.
Alleviate the mandate that I forgive you.
It will not happen.

Take me to a world without pain,
I don't want to hear any sound,
Everything is an intrusion.
Subject me not to your attempts at peace
making.
We need not speak again.

www.josieyoung.com

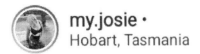

my.josie ·
Hobart, Tasmania

⋮

I cannot bear the thought of you,
I wish you death, pain and hurt,
You can't wait this one out –
My mind will not change.

Remember the night?
So many years ago –
When you raped me
...and laughed at your 'win' –
That laugh...

www.josieyoung.com

my.josie •
Hobart, Tasmania

I hope you remember it
Because my dream is to ensure...,
Ensure it is your last.

www.josieyoung.com

petren33 ·

He who laughs the loudest,
Who smiles the brightest,
Who brings so much joy,
Is the happiest right?
Well, you might be wrong,
Because the happier they act
The more they might be trying to cover up the
hurt and the pain,
Inside they're going insane,
But they don't want to show it,
They know people care,
But they couldn't bear being a burden,
Putting their troubles on others,
A smile can cover so much,
So don't always believe what you see,
It might not be as true and as real as it may
seem.

@petren33

israelmgonzalez ·

⋮

He who laughs the loudest cries the softest
So said the wise man
The super man is the last man
The homebody the vagabond
Who settled in Alexandria the furthest
The warrior who found eternal peace
Far away from Olympus and its gods
In the east he put put his mind at ease
Laughing his damnation away
For in his sadness he find the happiness of the gods
Of Zeus and Hera and the shiny sprites
Far in their galaxy long leagues away
Staring down upon he who laughs the loudest
And cries the softest

— Izzy Levy

 writing_mode ·

HE WHO LAUGHS LOUDEST..

Momentary Imprintings , that left a permanent mark..
Time when innocence was brutally barked..
Those compassionate hands made a spark,
And left out alone in that pitch black dark..

Thus you were agonized to go for the
search, see if that feel is still your's ?
Even if not, tell them how much they have been lured..
Capture them forcibly and trap in your world,
You need them most, so they have to dissolve.. !!

All they should talk with and all they should touch,
You shall be the destination with your fallen leaves of love
The clarifying intensions very proudly say,
You love them the most, then why not they ?

He who laughs loudest , just have a think,
Locked up identity has turned throughout slink..
The hands you crave for are no more affine,
They wish to run out of this dark bitched swine..

The caged identity has turned into the chains,
Whom you fonded are served with pain..
Your obsession can't find a justified bail,
You are the victim, who opted the sinner's trail..

wildernest_poetry
The Woods

scorned and pilloried/
they jeered at her fall
from grace/
free, she laughed loudest

Wildernest

@jmarie_voe

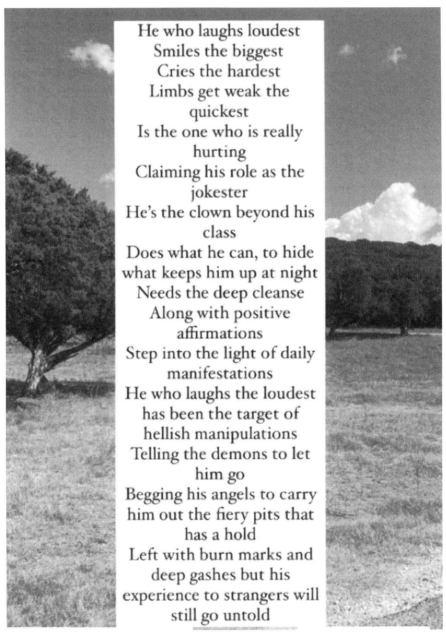

He who laughs loudest
Smiles the biggest
Cries the hardest
Limbs get weak the
quickest
Is the one who is really
hurting
Claiming his role as the
jokester
He's the clown beyond his
class
Does what he can, to hide
what keeps him up at night
Needs the deep cleanse
Along with positive
affirmations
Step into the light of daily
manifestations
He who laughs the loudest
has been the target of
hellish manipulations
Telling the demons to let
him go
Begging his angels to carry
him out the fiery pits that
has a hold
Left with burn marks and
deep gashes but his
experience to strangers will
still go untold

JEALOUSY

crystallotus759 ·

JEALOUSY

Jealousy makes its home in my selfish mind,
my unpleasant emotions making me blind ,
hurt others sentiments, I am not that kind,
feel insecure when anyone better than me I find .

Synonyms of sadness, antonyms of happiness,
make my close friends cry with my rudeness,
burning internally in the flame of covetousness,
I weep silently for being lost in my self created darkness.

crystallotus

 a_c_lawless ·

⋮

Jealousy

Jealousy:
An ugly trait
that lives and
breathes in all of
us, that every
so often, unleashes
a loathsome
feeling extending
from one individual
to another,
eventually consuming
our lives.
We want and want,
many times,
what we'll never
get.
And yet...

Jealousy:
Nothing flattering
about it;
A heinous need
to possess
The lure of the
forbidden
to see, watch
with desire
blinding, aching,
An addictive drug.
And we ignore
the consequences,
a pure quality that
corrodes us
slowly.
If only...

@a_c_lawless

 beboldtoya ·

watch me
****

I
VOW to be dismissive
of
M
Y
earthly judges
It is easy to assume the role of a spectator
and JUDGE
just because
God is my JUDGE
I am
no longer rattled by the critics
hissing like a snake
with venom on
their TOngues
JUDGIng me based on their
experiences
their
Insecurities
J
E
A
LO
U
S
Y

Fear
Hatred
whatever their reasons
I pray for them
sadly being judgmental
appears to be a human trait
I won't JUDGE you
for JUDGING me
I think humans are wired critics
I am not here to impress
I am here to express myself
I urge you to continue
JUDGING me
after-all life is one big stage
enjoy my act
grab some popcorn
watch me glow up
watch me blow up
J
U
D
G
E
at your leisure
For Pleasure

@beboldtoya

 adanakaz_poetry ·

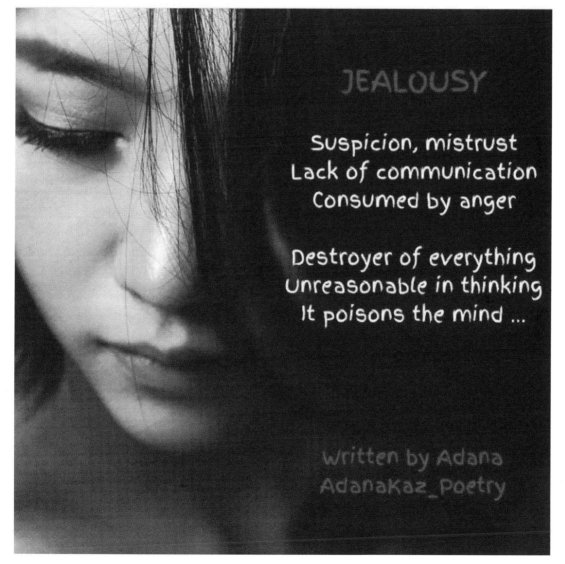

poetry_ordeal_solitude_solace_ · ⋮

Jealousy is a poison
That can rust even stainless strings
And golden ties, severing deep bonds
Render bottomless feelings
Make our minds restless, vanishing smiles
A wilting flower in springtime
Awkwardness in atmosphere
Faking it all like a poser
It's a venomous potion
Once you gulp in, you're done for
It eats up your insides, no more in control
There's no going back then, even if you want now
Cause you ruined heavens into hell for yourself
Where happiness lived, there now hatred dwells

©HIDDEN DEMOISELLE (jealousy)

ERUPTION

 **patriciahelenwriter** ⋅

ERUPTION

At first... all is calm.

What was that?
Did you hear it?

It's nothing at all.

Was that a thump?
Did something fall?

There you go again
you and your imagination!

Just listen for a minute.
This needs investigation.

RUMBLE...RUMBLE...RUMBLE
CRASH...WHOOSH...ROAR...

Guess you're right!
Hang on tight!
Must be a plumbing obstruction
or a frigging water tank eruption!

Good God... look over there!
Water's gushing everywhere!

poet_in_the_wilderness ·   ⋮

Time is ticking
Hear it pass in the
steady beat of
incessant storms
Dripping ever closer
to Autumn's explosion
Trees bursting into flame
Rocking in the aftermath
Their tops flickering with fire

Nothing to do but watch
as the city burns
Shedding it's skin
dried and crumbling
Embers drifting on the wind
igniting everything in their path
Making way for the descent of
white December ash
A cold reminder
of what the year has cost

Ending one cycle
yet ushering in another
Heavy clouds spilling
hopeful tears from the sky
onto ground that has been
burnt before

But still
it trusts the promise
of a new year to come
bringing Spring's

Gentle Renewal
@Poet_in_the_Wilderness

poet_ry_pot ·
Heraklion, Greece

Give me a fire,
flames that will stay.
Give me a fire,
I won't ask you for water.
Dawn's first cold is breaking out,
in a city that no one is awake
and the houses are trapped
in deep deep sleep.
The sun comes out in pinks,
violets and blues.
Your warm scent,
taking over my nostrils.
Colours reflected on your face.
A sentimental eruption.

Katerina Kozi

maria_at_40 · ⋮

The news has dried up,
so it's time to disrupt.
They've tales to construct
and a public to bluff.
Catastrophise stuff,
until it gets rough.
Watch the crowds rush,
the dunce and the mug.
A shove and a push,
another concussed.
The rest of us judge
these self centred thugs.
The media smug
as the panic erupts.

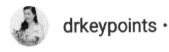 drkeypoints ·

Talked like a lamb whose voice was affable and innocent
Consumed eight hours straight in meditation and adoration
Each word in the holy book was understood and well lived
Until mouth got cursed into Pharisean's lips.
Fast for days,
Altar full of dianthuses
Served as a crutches to the uniped
But eyes belittle the sinners.
A sleeping lamb would caress the heavens
but when heart's impure would unleash ravens
Thou shall not worship in silence , with half-boiled soul and
wonders of devotion
For saints that deny to carry sinner's cross would wake hell's
eruption.

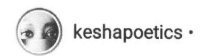 keshapoetics ·   ⋮

We kissed the words
When we spoke them
Leaning on an evening
Not meant for our bodies
Feared by their minds
Stop and gawk
But you will lose every time
At the waiting game
Stringing pretty syllables
Decorate the square
You've banned us
We come roaring back
Tasting your hatred   confrontation
Like hungry wolves

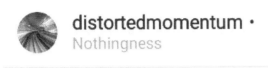

distortedmomentum ⋅

Nothingness

⋮

In an ocean of nothingness
We search through the words
Seeking for connection in an absurdly
social world

distortedmomentum

@jmarie_voe

In this Lovely Volcanic Eruption
I would die for you
I'm not you're lover
Friend or neighbor
But a guardian angel
Who's fallen into this environment
Learning crucial information before our paths ever crossed
And still this angel felt drawn to the one who was really lost
Teaching you what real love and loyalty was
Accepted all your beastly features with open arms
You were lost within your thoughts and feelings of the angel you were
seeing
I was getting shot with everyone's hateful bullets
And would start bleeding
Each one left me scarred and yet I wasn't complaining
I felt they were worth taking, because the connection I held with you
was worth more
Than anybody's basic narrow minded thinking
But I was dying slowing
All while in another direction you started pulling
I was meant to die for the one who was written in my scriptures...it was
YOU
A Deadly Devotion
Volcanic Eruption
Sacrificed my reputation for your protection

REBEL MIND

lismcdermott ·

A rebel mind, is something we should all encourage
to develop a way of thinking , a vouce of your own kind.
The ability to think outside the box, with anyone engage,
Showing you have the intelligence to use your own mind.

Free speech is the luxury of living within a democratic
society, telling lies, hiding secrets, sharing truths,
Possibilites endless, you can spout anything fantastic,
Even shout down the government from the tallest roofs.

A rebel mind would not last long, dwelt in a dictatorship
Their song would be quietened, their lips permanently sealed,
Likely, they would be sentenced to many lashes of the whip
Their critical words, tip-toeing through a constant minefield.

© Lis McDermott 2021

patriciahelenwriter ·

REBEL MIND

Restless spirit
Encaged in routine
Becomes agitated
Envisions new scene
Lifting limitations.

Marching forward
Intending change.
Never gives up.
Determined gains.

poet_ry_pot ·
Heraklion, Greece

Hands lean on absolution.
Holding rocks,
letting go sand,
atoms crashing.
Glorifying an unknown colour.
My mind cannot reverse it.
My rebel mind.

Katerina Kozi

 israelmgonzalez ·

He's A Rebel

He holds no gun in hand
He's leading no merry, merry band
He's a rebel
He's a lonesome rebel

He's in search for some portal to a new dawn
He's always gotta have the light on
He's a rebel
He's a lonesome rebel

He stares insistently at a distant galaxy
He's in communion with the old man and the sea
He's a rebel
He's a lonesome rebel

He's occupied with sizing infinities
With directions and with cardinalities
He's a rebel
He's a lonesome rebel

He's living in a world that they can't understand
He's a charlatan they say throughout the land
He's a rebel
He's a lonesome rebel
©israelmgonzalez

 m.meanders ·

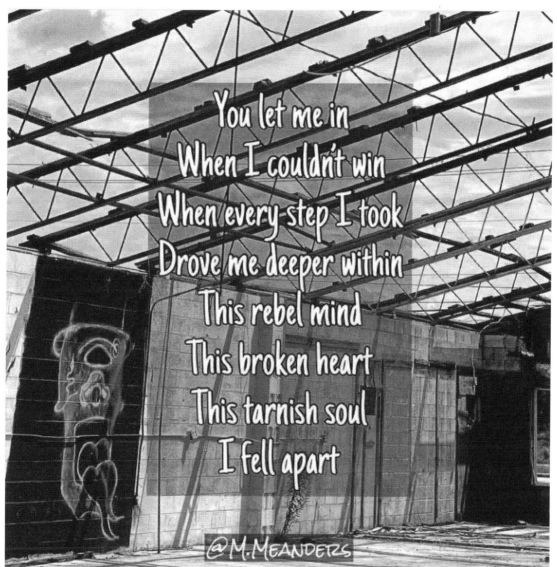

 jaimeboey

Flesh once
exuberantly held, then withered
to threadbare bones;
I dreamt of love, savored then crushed
my soul to shreds;
Shackled heart of a fallen angel wept in dire
Lived a blue-eyed on chariot clouds of fire

Mired amongst rainstorm disruptors
patience to new wings feathers her worth
To possess will be your eyes of poetries
so tell me your sweet little fears;
I looked to the sky for answers when it's laid deep in my heart
I don't know of your riddles to make these glass slippers fit

Hazed beyond illusioned depths of muddy waters
Despondent screams to be out of stagnancy
I'm choked by its obsessive grip to break free
Whirling reel in continuous fanciful replay

She was god-stained and hell made
so gently my foaming fingers embraced
emancipation of my rebel mind.

@JAIMEBOEY

@jmarie_voe

Rebel mind one of a kind
Spiritually intimidating
Rebelling against the
pressures to cut and slice
my body open
For the empty souls that'll
fill mine with toxic wasteful
ideas that I need to spread
myself thin
All while drinking my pure
blood I once had pumping
through my veins
No sir that is ill
misrepresentation
Don't obey the rules
Rebel till the death of me
Venom killing negative
energy
Can't tame me I run free
I'll be a rebel for all eternity
Bold and Outstanding
Call it that vibe over
everything
Falling out of order
unapologetically

EMANCIPATION

 lismcdermott ·

Eman[anating a sense of complete freedom, allows for mindful anti]cipation.

 debbie_o_bottled_up_feelings ·

i no longer care
what you may think of me
i no longer care
if my face and body
please you
cause i'm pleasing myself
and everything i do now
is myself loving me
cause i've lived without that
far to long
some may say i'm selfish
but
if you want something done
you must do it yourself
so i'm loving me
let's be clear
it's the emancipation
of me

debbie o bottled up feelings

 life_begets_here ·

Unaddressed letter to the Dawn //

Under the canopies and the tender foliages
Are fallen absolutely like leaves of love,
After being osculated by morning sunbeams and
blue morning rays,
Revamping the gloomy sky with dispersed clouds
into a trawny sheet of quilt;
Indicating that change is coming, and ultimately
resulting in emancipation,
Soaring birds chattered that dawn is a
quintessential hope,
That illuminates every beautiful soul's sugary smile,
And absolute unadulterated caressing nature,
As warm and inevitable as the dawn in our
Macrocosm.

~Divya R Reddy

// @life_begets_here

alison.paige ·

⋮

Second star to the Right and straight on till morning.

The land of fairies and flying and never growing up.

Everything is pretend but it's home to the

emancipated children of never-neverland.

The heaven-esque island may seem sweet until

Peter thins the lost boys out. ⟫⟫⟫⟫——————⟶

Go far away from hangman's tree, for Hook is not

the villain of this tale. ⟵——————⟪⟪⟪

@_alison.paige_

beboldtoya
Freedom

⋮

Freedom

engulfed in a plethora
of cultural norms
I
identified
with the quintessential
expectations
of an Island Country
G
I
R
L
conflicted
torn
as I matured
with
M
Y
exposure
through travels
or books read
M
Y
awareness came alive

and
prompted
a constant battle
to finding my identity
enslaved by
M
Y
fears
M
Y
blissful ignorance
and
imposed guilt
I performed
until
July 2017
when
I
emancipated myself
from expectations
and mental slavery

@beboldtoya

 taratalksthoughts

Eyes consider possibility
Heart squeezes open with hope
Warms up my body and soul
Life can happen, Not in this moment but the
future lacks freezing cold
Happy to reflect
That this power came to interject
Door's open, maybe's ajar
Hope has brought me back to life
on our journey so far

@jmarie_voe

Join hands
Bow your heads
Let us pray
For better days
Open your hearts
To receive
An anointing and
anonymous breeze
Let it take you into the
forest of your dreams
Becoming one with
nature
Until breath leaves the
body permanently
And your soul begins to
fly freely effortlessly

DEEP LONGING

 petren33 ·   ⋮

I have a deep longing for a feeling of belonging,
To find a place where I fit perfectly,
No manipulation or change needed,
I just get seeded in place
And easily find my pace,
Fitting in perfectly,
Growing with everyone around me,
Seeing everyone show their real and true selves,
One day I hope to find my place,
Somewhere I don't face any resistance,
I can just persist on and be myself,
With no feeling of any need to shove parts of me
away on a shelf,
Hopefully one day I find a place where I belong
perfectly,
I guess I'll just have to wait and see.

@petren33

 emm_kay0 ·

A deep longing

For the sound of the waves crashing,
crashing throughout the night just out-
side rushing, rushing across the tide,the
surf dancing, dancing in sheer delight
rising falling rising falling rising again
singing, singing with waves singing with
stars singing with mermaids caressing,
caressing the sands holding, holding
them in their arms playfully teasing,
teasing each other shining, shining glim-
mering glittering with a silver light mes-
merizing, mesmerizing the moon in thrall
enchanting, enchanting it along with me.
©emm_kay

 **realmpoetry** ·

⋮

Those who fall in love
Is like a butterfly
Longing for deep love
Saving their last breathe
Consume their pride
And when they ready
Their shades will explode

Realm

poetry_ordeal_solitude_solace_ ·

Deep longing

I told you that I've been told
I need you to know that I needed
you to know
I wanted to say that you should've
said

But now, am I too late to tell you
that you're too late?
Have I held on too long to let you
know your time has passed?
Did I forget to ask you whether you
forgot to ask me?

It's coming to me;
Now that I've waited long enough for
you to stop waiting
Now that I've been told by someone
who didn't wait so long
Now that you just live in my worse
memories of longing

Hasn't it occurred to you yet?
You've been long forgotten by me who
never once forgot the touch of
your fingertips

© HIDDEN
DEMOISELLE

sticksandstonespoet ·
Melbourne, Victoria, Australia

sitting on my shoulder whispering in my ear
you're my every self doubt
my every fear my every failure
your pulling me under
and I'm never enough never enough
ohh dear anxiety it's you again
biting my ankles crippling me
I can't move on I need release
from this self destructing entity
residing in my head ohh dear anxiety
I need to learn to live.. without you
you take my words each time
your hands choking my self worth until I am
blue
with every death I die a little more inside

@sticksandstonespoet
©dmccarthy

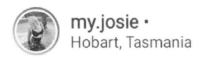

my.josie •
Hobart, Tasmania

I long to be the one your very essence cannot be without.

I want every particle of you yearning to connect to me.

May your senses feel nothing but dullness.

Any time you are pulled away from me.

Want me so passionately the tides turn

as the moon strains to see our love...

Give me a love more vast it disparages the ocean.

Warm my soul more than the sun warms the earth.

Touch me all over like you are the wind

and I am a cloud floating on your breath.

Breath me in. Let me fill your lungs.

And give you life – and fulfil my purpose.

Long for me so deeply.

That the ocean is shamed by your depths.

Long for me like I long for you...

WWW.JOSIEYOUNG.COM

thedarksideofthephoenix ·

Do you hear the sirens call, drifting on the winds of time?
The sweet melody of my soul, calling you home.
Wondering if you feel regret, if you will ever atone,
You told me that your mistakes, you would own.
You penned your thoughts with bravery,
And I believed the words that you sent to me.
You swore to rectify the hurt & the lies,
Looked deep into my forlorn eyes.
Promised me that you would not justify,
The pain you had caused me, you'd rather die.
You identified what you needed to do,
Communicate, be vulnerable, & have patience too.
You said that it was all worth it because,
Of the deep longing & love, that you had for me,
Needing me to be yours for eternity.
You would atone, you gave me your guarantee,
But none of it was real, this I see,
And now i'm paying the price for my stupidity...

 cleopatrafernhill1   ⋮

When A Cold Heart Melts
Darkness dissolves when a cold heart melts,
moon wrestles with billowy clouds forming above,
molded by the midnight hour and sweet dreams of
yearnings now awakened, ripening, responding.
Countless diamonds carefully arranged in the night sky
become a canopy of light,
a stairway to the moon and all his secrets
he's been yearning to reveal
like celestial love letters from the cosmos.
I whisper my secrets to full moon rising,
his warmth of moonbeams cascading onto
slow touches,
a matchbox of wishes, desires,
like meteors lighting up the sky,
like rays of sunlight after countless nights of rain
sizzling now in moments of delight.

© *Cleo 2021*
@cleopatrafernhill1

 cleopatrafernhill1

⋮

Each word is warm sunshine on my skin,
a lighthouse beckoning you to me,
carried by midnight, summer breezes,
transcending, stroking, swaying,
creating rhythms of delight, pathways to our hearts,
foretold in constellations, radiant,
become a universe of their own.
Abandoning fear, he made me believe in the impossible,
made me dream again.
He asked me,
"What do you want from me, my love?"
I gazed into his eyes and replied,
"Everything, absolutely everything!
I want all of you, every single part of you, my love.
I want all of you."
© Cleo 2021
@cleopatrafernhill1

@jmarie_voe

Deep longing to run in a field filled
with sunflowers and butterflies
Sun light on the eyes is heavy
But breathing in fresh air is alright
with me
It's a lovely day to dance and sing
It's a lovely day for us to be in unity
Fishing on the lakeside
Radio playing mellow tunes our paddle
boats set to the side
No fantasy that was once lovely
It's now our own beautiful reality
It's a lovely day to be alive
It's a lovely day to be free of society's
shackles holy tide
Deep longing to remember what
summer feels like
To chase the clouds cute picnic set up
lounging by the lakeside
Spinning in a field filled with weeping
willow trees and fireflies

ABOUT THE CURATOR

"Like some kind of semi-aquatic mammal, I've always felt I don't quite fit in, and I struggle to swim in certain streams for too long. I'm certainly not the most adaptable or flexible soul, and sometimes you'll spot me, clinging stubbornly to my clumsy armbands and hoping for the best. Try as I might, I'm always halfway in-between. But I do have a certain luminosity about me; my character dances from time to time, and ever occasionally, my personality shines through and sticks in people's minds. I have an aura of sorts and as a writer, artist and human, I hope that counts for something."

RDW

Ryan Daniel Warner, is a self-styled 'Writer, Artist and Human' hailing from Northern England - the 'Lake District' to be precise. He owns the Instagram account, @rdw.world, and the website www.rdw.world, which both showcase his various projects related heavily to poetry, writing and wordplay.

His debut work, 'Book One' – the first in an ongoing, life-long 100-part series is now available to purchase on Amazon and via his website. 'Book Two' is on its way (it's now way more than fashionably late). In addition, 'White Book' – the first in a series of 'Colours' will also be available "soon," while this 'Poetry 365' anthology is released each month, featuring the work of a very talented collection of poets that become involved with his poetry prompts on Instagram.

Ryan would also like you to know that he hates speaking in third person about himself, or pretending that somebody else has written the above, so he will end this anthology, characteristically, in first person by simply saying

Thank you to all involved.
To those who wrote such wonderful pieces,
and to those who had the pleasure of reading them.

PLEASE SHOW YOUR SUPPORT FOR THE AMAZING POETS INVOLVED IN THIS EDITION OF 'POETRY 365' BY FOLLOWING THEM ON INSTAGRAM AND CHECKING OUT THEIR WORK.

Printed in Great Britain
by Amazon

68624938R00158